Carnations
and Pinks

Pamela McGeorge and Keith Hammett

Principal photographer Russell McGeorge

FIREFLY BOOKS

Acknowledgments

Writing a book of this nature draws on the knowledge and expertise of many gardeners. In particular, the authors and the photographer would like to thank Brian and Meg Claxton of Bay Bloom Nurseries and Ian Duncalf of Parva Plants; also Sarah Hodge and Wayne Horrobin, all of whom gave us free rein to photograph their extensive collections of dianthus. Special thanks are due to Pat Stuart. Her garden is inspirational and gave us many happy hours of wandering and photographing. We are grateful to other gardeners also, too numerous to name, whose enchanting plantings of dianthus inspired photographs. We are indebted to Dennis Chatfield who shared his love of perpetual carnations with us, to our favorite florist Jacque Holbrook, who created a spectacular floral arrangement for inclusion in the book, to Yoshito Iwasa of Yokohama, Japan for much assistance in researching the history of the Ise dianthus and to Professor Brian Murray of Auckland, New Zealand for facilitating cytogenetic research into the genus. Our grateful thanks also to Tracey Borgfeldt, who initiated the project and encouraged us along the way.

Photographs on pages 13 (top), 19, 20, 21 (left), 24, 26, 27, 34, 37, 38 (left), 41 (left), 44, 56 (upper), 68, 85–88 by Dr. Keith Hammett.

Front cover: Main photo, 'Front Cover', bred by Dr. Keith Hammett (photo K. Hammett).
Page 1: Simple, uncomplicated old pink.
Page 2: Roses and pinks have a timeless appeal.
Page 3: 'Polly', a pretty, perfumed, miniature pink.

A FIREFLY BOOK

Published by Firefly Books Ltd. 2002

Copyright © 2002 Pamela McGeorge, Keith Hammett and David Bateman Ltd

First Printing

National Library of Canada Cataloguing in Publication Data

McGeorge, Pamela, 1943–
    Carnations and pinks
Includes index.
ISBN 1-55297-554-1 (bound)   ISBN 1-55297-553-3 (pbk.)
1. Carnations. 2. Pinks. I. Hammett, Keith II. McGeorge, Russell, 1943–III. Title.
SB413.C3M33 2002   635.9'3353   C2001-901802-9

U.S. Cataloging-in-Publication Data (Library of Congress Standards)

McGeorge, Pamela
    Carnations and pinks / Pamela McGeorge ; Keith
Hammett ; photographs by Russell McGeorge.—1st ed.
[96] p. : col. photos. ; cm.
Includes index.
Summary: Guide to using and growing carnations and pinks in your garden.
Includes design ideas, sources and directory of carnations and pinks.
ISBN 1-55297-554-1
ISBN 1-55297-553-3 (pbk.)
1. Carnations. 2. Pinks. I. Hammett, Keith. II. McGeorge, Russell. III. Title.
635.93353 21 CIP SB413.C3.M34 2002

Published in Canada in 2002 by Firefly Books Ltd., 3680 Victoria Park Avenue, Willowdale, Ontario M2H 3K1

Published in the United States in 2002 by Firefly Books (U.S.) Inc., P.O. Box 1338, Ellicott Station, Buffalo, New York 14205

Cover design Shelley Watson/Sublime Design; Design Errol McLeary; Typesetting Jazz Graphics, Auckland
Printed in Hong Kong through Colorcraft Ltd

Contents

Introduction

Early summer. A warm, calm evening and the air is redolent with the sweet, spicy perfume of pinks. Dianthus grow in my garden where the climate is Mediterranean—hot and dry in summer, frosty cold in winter. The soil is gravelly and huge chunks of schist add impressive character to the landscape. Dianthus love it. They grow wild among the rough stones; they tumble down rock walls; they thrive alongside sage and thyme and their blue-gray-silver foliage shimmers in the heat of midday. I love them for their variety, for their limitless shades of pink, and above all for their timeless perfume that stirs the senses and creates links between gardeners in other times and other places. For carnations and pinks, both members of the *Dianthus* family, are flowers that our grandmothers grew, that gardeners in the western world have cherished for centuries.

As early as the 1500s, enthusiastic growers in Europe collected dianthus. They bred them, traded them, painted them and wrote about them. The plants traveled. Adventurers, out to conquer new worlds, brought back "new" species from Asia. Colonists introduced them to the New World. The gene pool grew and the quest continued. Enthusiasts were forever seeking yet a newer variety, yet another color combination. Artisans bred them to exhibit at shows, where the flowers had to meet rigorous standards. Growers with an eye for commercial possibilities developed the genus to produce the quintessential flower for floral display.

Until this century, the history of carnations and pinks has been intertwined with social customs of the day. As they followed the roller coaster of fashion, new varieties emerged, old ones were lost and even many of the species have been submerged in the confusion of multiple varieties that are often very similar.

With a genus so variable, it is important that distinct characteristics should be preserved even while new attributes are sought. This is the task of dianthus breeders today. One is Dr. Keith Hammett, who has filled the role of specialist consultant for this book and contributed the chapter on hybridizing. He fell in love with carnations as a young boy in England where he exhibited flowers he had raised himself. As a young man he made his home in New

Left: 'Valda Wyatt'
Opposite: 'Alan Titchmarsh'

Cerinthe major (honeywort) and 'Doris'.

Zealand and has since become world-renowned as a plant breeder. *Dianthus* has been one of his specialties for several decades; first, he worked with border carnations, more recently, with garden pinks. He has been in the forefront of the recent research aimed at producing a yellow-flowering dianthus with attractive blooms and a tidy garden habit. He continues to hybridize, following a breeding program to develop new plants with repeat-flowering ability, distinct patterns and interesting color.

When you go to this breeder's garden, you see row after long row of carefully cultivated dianthus, each slightly different, each in the process of being carefully assessed for its future as a marketable garden plant. Some of these dianthus are covered in blooms. I covet them, but Keith warns me this is only their first year. Wait and see, he cautions—wait and see what next year brings.

Today, carnations are predominantly flowers for professional florists; the pinks, in their ever-chang-

ing variety, are the flowers that gardeners love. Their combined story is a fascinating one. In the following pages we bring you the history of these plants, details of their progression over the years and new information about recent cultivars and the people who have developed them. We talk about how to grow them and suggest ideas for using them in your garden.

Popular cultivars mentioned in the book were available at the time of writing, but many are ephemeral. We suggest you consider color and patterning, as well as the size and habit of the variety, when deciding on the planting scheme for your garden, then consult nurseries and seed sellers for details about the dianthus they are offering at any particular time, and match them to your wants.

Plant them, admire them and enjoy their perfume.

Hardiness Zone Map

This map has been prepared to agree with a system of plant hardiness zones that have been accepted as an international standard and range from 1 to 11. It shows the minimum winter temperatures that can be expected on average in different regions.

In this book, where a zone number has been given, the number corresponds with a zone shown here. That number indicates the coldest areas in which the particular plant is likely to survive through an average winter. Note that these are not necessarily the areas in which it will grow best. Because the zone number refers to the minimum temperatures, a plant given zone 7, for example, will obviously grow perfectly well in zone 8, but not in zone 6. Plants grown in a zone considerably higher than the zone with the minimum winter temperature in which they will survive might well grow but they are likely to behave differently. Note also that some readers may find the numbers a little conservative; we felt it best to err on the side of caution.

°F	Zone	°C
below -50	1	below -45
-50 to -40	2	-45 to -40
-40 to -30	3	-40 to -34
-30 to -20	4	-34 to -29
-20 to -10	5	-29 to -23
-10 to 0	6	-23 to -16
0 to 10	7	-16 to -12
10 to 20	8	-12 to -7
20 to 30	9	-7 to -1
30 to 40	10	-1 to 4
above 40	11	above 4

Hardiness zones are based on
the average annual minimum
temperature for each zone.

CHAPTER 1

Outline of the Genus

Plants, like people, form naturally occurring groups that share similar characteristics. And as with people, plants need names that identify them and link them to others in the same family. The Greeks and Romans originated the system of naming plants by including descriptive details in their title, but it was Carl Linnaeus, a Swedish botanist in the 18th century, who devised the less cumbersome classification system still used today.

Instead of the descriptive phrases used by herbalists and botanists of his day, Linnaeus gave each plant two names in Latin form. The first is the word for the genus—equivalent to our surname—and the second is a specific description, such as our given name. Together they provide a name by which this particular plant species is universally known.

In the centuries since Linnaeus, botanists have continued to develop his system of plant classification. The entire plant kingdom is divided and subdivided into a multibranched "family tree," according to each plant's characteristics. As new discoveries are made, or more precise analyses become possible, botanists sometimes rename plants or reclassify their family connections—to the continuing frustration of gardeners.

The broadest grouping to which a plant belongs is the **family**, similar to a human clan, and this is determined by the structure of the flowers, the fruits and other parts of the plant. So the genus *Dianthus* belongs to the larger family of Caryophyllaceae and includes the tall-stemmed, highly bred, many-petaled carnations we know from the florist's shop, as well as the sweet-smelling pinks, well loved by generations of cottage gardeners. Within any plant

Above: Textures of velvet and taffeta.
Opposite: Clove-scented 'Becka Falls' would have seemed very familiar to gardeners of the 16th century.

family there may be one genus or many, and *Lychnis, Silene* and *Gypsophila* are genera, related to *Dianthus*, also belonging to Caryophyllaceae. Next time you see *Gypsophila*, take a close look at the tiny flowers and see how they resemble those of their big cousin, the carnation. *Lychnis* and *Silene*, on the other hand, have single, five-petaled flowers that resemble the shape of the flowers of old pinks.

Within each **genus** there may be one or many **species**. Carnation or pink, all those we know today have been bred from various species of *Dianthus* that

Above: A subtle beauty, 'Pink Monica Wyatt'.

originated in central and southern Europe and Asia. Carnations, it is thought, are descended from the species *Dianthus caryophyllus* and have 30 chromosomes; pinks are derived from the species *D. plumarius* and, curiously, though they appear less complicated, have 90 chromosomes.

An individual plant may be a **variety**, which, strictly speaking, occurs naturally and is defined by botanists as a **taxon** below species level. Alternatively, it may be a **cultivar**, which is a variant resulting from human activity. (Common usage has cultivar and **variety** as being interchangeable.) Species will come true to type from seed; cultivars must be propagated by cuttings or other vegetative means to retain their genetic structure.

Dianthus caryophyllus carries the genes for the characteristic clove scent of the traditional carnation. It also brings to the genus tall, upright growth; thick, strong flower stems with long spaces between the joints or **nodes**; and often double flowers, usually bigger than those of pinks and in almost every color

except blue. These are the attributes that have been so important for the carnation as a cut flower. Among the genus *Dianthus* are five main types:

Border carnations have a long ancestry in Europe. Many named cultivars have come and gone over the centuries, and in the days when carnation shows were popular, prizes for the best border carnations were hotly contested. Victims of declining fashion and because they need staking, border carnations are not widely grown now. Nevertheless, they are hardy (though short-lived) perennials that will survive in zone 3, where temperatures sometimes plummet to -40°F (-40°C).

Annual carnations are popular throughout North America. They flower prolifically right through summer, with blooms generally smaller than those of the border carnations, and although they will overwinter in mild climates, they are usually treated as annuals and planted from seed each year.

Perpetual-flowering carnations, those we buy from florists, made their appearance more recently. They first came on the market around 1850 and were bred to produce blooms for the cut-flower trade. These carnations are raised mainly by commercial growers and, in greenhouses where they usually grow, they will continue flowering all winter provided the temperature falls no lower than 50°F (10°C).

Pinks are well-loved garden plants, widely grown and cherished for their dainty flowers, often delicious perfume and their attractive blue-gray foliage that usually forms a low-growing, neat clump. The stems of pinks are thinner and shorter than those of carnations; the flowers may be single or double, fringed or rounded and they come in every color except blue and yellow.

Sweet Williams, vivid and summer-flowering, are also part of the *Dianthus* family. Dwarf or taller-

Above: Dianthus come in many guises.

growing varieties all bear dense clusters of brilliantly colored blooms on stout stems. When sweet Williams are in full flower, the bright green leaves become almost obscured.

The name of the genus was derived from two small Greek words—*Dios*, meaning divine, and *anthos*, flower. It is believed that Theophrastus, a pupil of Aristotle, in about 300 BC dedicated the flowers to Zeus, the most powerful deity in the line-up of Greek gods, but the early history of *Dianthus* is uncertain and the first steps in their evolution unknown.

Linnaeus was the first to describe the genus, in 1753. By 1893 more than 230 species had been described, but of this number very few are of any importance to gardeners. Wildly promiscuous, the different species are notorious for their interbreeding and it is often difficult to trace the exact parentage of many hybrids. This is further complicated by the lack of a recent revision of the genus by taxonomists, and so today the plants available to gardeners bear a bewildering and constantly changing array of names.

Above: Sweet William has been cherished in cottage gardens for several hundred years.

CHAPTER 2

Plants with a Past

It's hardly a revolutionary theory that the urge to grow plants is one of the defining characteristics of being human—after all, the need for a reliable source of food could be called a strong incentive. But the history of humans is littered with evidence of plants grown purely for ornamental purposes, and to be a gardener is to automatically tap into that history. Every plant we grow today had its beginnings in some ancient species. The recorded history of pinks and carnations is not as venerable as that of some plants: there are no carvings of carnations on ancient Egyptian tombs, as there are of irises; pinks do not feature as architectural details on Greek columns, as do acanthus. After Theophrastus described the flower of dianthus in 300 BC, it disappeared again for more than 1000 years.

Some researchers believe that, because wild forms have been found in the Atlas Mountains, it is possible the Romans introduced the plant into Spain. It has been suggested that the plant came to England from Normandy with William the Conqueror and his camp. Certainly, in modern times, dianthus have been found growing wild on the ancestral castle walls at Falaise on the coast of Normandy, though this in no way constitutes proof. Others consider that dianthus could have been brought to Western Europe after 1353, when the Ottomans crossed the Dardanelles.

Their presence in an old painting of the English King Edward IV, who reigned in the 15th century, would seem to confirm that carnations grew in

Above: Astrantias and dianthus enjoy similar conditions.

English gardens then. But even this is disputed. Some writers tell you the picture plainly shows a rose, others swear it has to be a carnation. No matter, legends make for interesting conjecture. What we do know is that the earliest drawing of a pink discovered so far dates from 1415. It shows a single form of the flower. By 1450, illuminated art-

Opposite: Pinks like these have gladdened gardeners' hearts for centuries.

Above: Self-seeding and easy to maintain, these pinks create their own harmony.

is clove-scented with a Latin name that means clove-leafed and a common name that could easily be mistaken for *clou de girofle*, the French name for the culinary clove. Some say that Chaucer's mention of "clowe gelofre," used to sweeten ale in his *Canterbury Tales*, is evidence that dianthus grew in England in the 14th century. But French was still the language of the English court when Chaucer wrote his tales and it seems certain that he was in fact referring to the spice, especially as he writes of "clowe gelofre" in the same context as nutmeg.

Gillyflower (and all its various spellings) is confusing enough by itself. In the past it referred to several flowers. There was stock gillyflower, today known as stock; wall gillyflower, our wallflowers, and queen's gillyflower, now sweet rocket. "Gilly" or "jully" referred to July, the month when all these plants bloomed in the Northern Hemisphere.

works showed double and improved flower forms, indicating that by then human hands had taken part in its hybridization.

Between 1490 and 1510, dianthus appear more frequently in art. Double dianthus were frequently depicted on Persian tiles of the 16th century, they were mentioned in Eastern writings as early as 1515 and garden forms of dianthus were established in Turkey, the Middle East and also in Western Europe by 1500.

Dispute about the authenticity of the earlier stories has been increased by confusion over names that have evolved for these plants. The botanical name given to the ancestor of today's florist carnation is *Dianthus caryophyllus*. Prior to the 16th century the common name for all dianthus was "gillofloure" or "gillyflower." Gillyflowers were traditionally described as "clove-scented" and *caryophyllus* means "clove-leafed" in Latin. However, the culinary clove *Eugenia aromatica* is sometimes known as *Caryophyllus aromatica*—more opportunity for confusion! So we have a flower that

In his *Herball*, published in 1597, where John Gerard discusses the genus, he states: "...some whereof are called Carnations, others Clove Gillofloures, some Sops in wine, some Pagiants..." In his descriptions, Gerard divides dianthus into three separate chapters headed: "Of Clove Gillofloures," "Of pinkes or wilde Gillofloures," and "Of Sweet Saint Johns and Sweet Williams."

Nor is the name "carnation" free of controversy. The form *incarnaycion* first appears in English in 1535 and was perhaps a corruption of the Latin word *coronaria*, signifying that dianthus flowers may have been used in coronets for festive occasions. But, again there is doubt. It has been suggested that carnation comes from the Latin *caro, carnis*, meaning flesh-colored. By 1597 the term carnation is in common use. Gerard describes the "great Carnation Gillo-floure with very fair floures of an excellent

sweet smell." William Shakespeare also talks about carnations in his plays. They feature in *Henry V* and *A Winter's Tale*:

> The fairest flowers o' the season
> Are our Carnations and streak'd Gillyflowers.

The name "pink" appeared first in English in 1573 and referred to the lower-growing plants with small flowers. It would seem, therefore, that during the 16th century gilliflower, carnation or pink had all become acceptable names for a genus that was well known in England and Western Europe, was grown in monastery and castle gardens and was valued for its perfume, when sweet-smelling herbs were necessary to mask the odors of the time. By then it was also evident from Gerard's writing that there were many varieties available and that every year, every climate and every country was bringing forth new kinds. They were prized for their colorings and markings as well as their scent—especially after the advent of laced pinks.

Above: 'Alice' is a perennial favorite.
Left: Well-loved, old-fashioned flowers.

1, Master Tuggie's Princess; 2, the French or Oxford Carnation; 3, the Westminster Gilloflower; 4, the Bristow Carnation; 5, the Chrystal or Chrystalline; 6, the Striped Sauadge; 7, the Granpere or Greatest Grenado; 8, the Dainty; 9, John Witty's Great Tawny Gilloflower; 10, the Stript Tawny; 11, the Marbled Tawny; 12, Mashe Tuggie's Rose Gilloflower. (From " Paradisus Terrestris.")

1, The Great Old Carnation or Gray Hulo; 2, the White Carnation; 3, the Camberwell or Poole Carnation; 4, the Fair Maid of Kent; 5, the Blush Sauadge; 6, the Gredeline; 7, the Grimelo or Prince; 8, the Great White Gilloflower; 9, Master Bradshawe's Dainty Lady.

Gerard mentions a yellow dianthus planted in his garden, given to him by a Polish merchant who had never before seen a yellow variety in England. John Parkinson, however, in his *Paradisi in Sole, Paradisus Terrestris*, published in 1629, indicates that yellow carnations had become popular toward the end of the previous century. He differentiates between gilloflowers with small blooms and carnations with larger blooms. He praises both gilloflowers and carnations for their variation, their perfume

Diagrams of carnations from the 17th-century book *Paradisi in Sole, Paradisus Terrestris.*

and their "bravery" and adds that there are so many known varieties it would be pointless to note them all with their individual differences.

Few references are found for the use of dianthus in herbal remedies, though it is thought that the Romans put the flowers in their wine to add to its flavor. A similar habit in the Middle Ages in

England was supposedly the source of the name for the old garden pink called sops-in-wine. Gerard talks of a conserve made of clove-scented pinks and sugar which "doth comfort the heart." Wild pinks, he noted, "...are not used in Physicke, but esteemed for their use in Garlands and Nosegaies."

English gardeners in the 17th century embraced the carnation with enthusiasm, though most stock was still accessed from Germany, Holland, Flanders and France. A catalog in 1676 listed 360 cultivars and by the end of the century, very large flowers in many colors were in great favor. Later still, and contrary to the idea of perfection today, the biggest bloom with the best burst calyx, called a "burster," was considered by some exhibitors to be the epitome of excellence. If the calyx did not burst, the bloom was called a "whole blower." Dedicated gardeners would take to the calyx with a sharp penknife or pair of scissors and do to the plant what nature had failed to do by itself. How surprised those enthusiasts of the past would be to learn that commercial growers nowadays buy small green plastic or cardboard "patches" designed to hold together any calyx that threatens to burst.

Flower-lovers through the ages have ranked carnations only second in universal favor to the rose. The American horticulturalist and author J. Harrison Dick, writing in 1915, says: "Although the flower may have its dark periods, when other favorites seem to crowd it a little and depreciate its value in the public eye, these are only temporary, and ...it will in the future, as for so many lifetimes behind us, remain one of the best beloved of all the flowers." Certainly the florists of the 18th century in England would have expressed similar views.

Preceding the Industrial Revolution, florists were not the flower sellers we think of today. They were flower breeders, selecting specimens with particular attributes and hybridizing them to produce "perfect" blooms to exhibit on the show bench. Many of these florists were Flemish and French weavers who had arrived in England, fleeing reli-

'Neat 'n' Tidy', a modern laced pink bred by Keith Hammett, reflects the black and white laced varieties loved by the florists of Paisley, Scotland in the 18th century.

gious persecution. They brought with them their artisan skills and their love of plants. Their everyday lives were spent at the loom; flowers were their hobby and their passion. Often they worked at home, in terraced houses with a tiny backyard where they raised their flowers and were always on hand to tend and cosset them. They exhibited their blooms at convivial "florists' feasts," held in inns, where the ale flowed and competition was fierce.

Along with anemones, auriculas, hyacinths, primroses, polyanthus, ranunculus and tulips, pinks and carnations became known as florists' flowers. Separate classifications were defined, fashions established. Flower characteristics were rigidly adhered to. "Painted ladies," which still exist today, have small, clove-scented flowers. Petals are pure white on the underside and look as if they have been brightly splashed with pink or red on the upper side.

These painted ladies were popular in the past—the commoners in the ranks—but they did not meet the exacting standards necessary to achieve *grande dame* status. The florists sought flowers more precisely marked, more aristocratically formed, circular in shape with smoothly rounded petals. "Piquettes," or "picotees" as they are now known, are characterized by a fine wire of contrasting color around the edge of each petal. John Galbally, well-known in the United Kingdom as a grower and breeder of *Dianthus* in the 20th century, reports in *Carnations and Pinks for Garden and Greenhouse* that the first picotee recorded, named 'Fair Helena', dates from 1683 and was described as "only edged with purple." Some early piquettes included spots and stripes on the petals—markings judged undesirable as the type became more refined.

"Flakes" displayed one contrasting color on a white background (also called "ground"), "bizarres" two or more distinct contrasting colors on a white ground. As exhibitors and breeders became more fanatic, these flakes, or wedge-shaped splashes of color radiating out from the center on a show bloom, had to be arranged in very particular ways or the bloom was considered imperfect.

By the 19th century, such was the emphasis on show blooms that plants were fed rich, potent manure to try and achieve ever larger flowers. These were "dressed" for exhibition. Specially shaped cards were made to hold the blooms in place and metal tweezers were used to tweak the calyx, turning back its points. Any defective petals were removed. Ivory tweezers were reserved for the more intricate business of rearranging the petals, drawing

A Group of old flaked and bizarre carnations. A reconstruction from a sketch by Samuel S. Moreton, c.1845

Above: Idealized Bizarres of the 19th century.

the outer layer further outward to increase the size of the bloom and gently persuading the inner layers to display their color patterns in the approved manner.

So intense was the competition, that some exhibitors in the north of England went to the length of employing a barber-wigmaker to dress their competition entries. It was rumored that his business in carnations was at least as remunerative as his business of dressing wigs. Intriguing to wonder if his clients turned up on his doorstep with a wig in one hand and a carnation bloom in the other.

The tradition of carnation shows with their strict requirements continued to be popular through many years of the 19th century in England, but as the traditional weaver-florists were absorbed into

DOUGLAS BORDER CARNATIONS

Orpheus	Bookham Lad
Albatross	Nell Gwynne
Beverley	Conachar

Above: Border carnations from a 1950s catalog.

Episcopal Church in Grafton, West Virginia. In a telegram to the congregation she stated that: "Each one present will be given a white carnation; mothers will be given two, in memory of the day."

Miss Jarvis gave the flowers in remembrance of her own mother, who had given long service to the church. She asked that everyone wear the flower and consider it as an emblem of purity, strength and endurance, symbols of ideal motherhood. The following year she sent 700 carnations on Mother's Day, and over time her gift to the church amounted to more than 10,000 carnations.

In today's world Miss Anna Jarvis could have been a marketer of genius. Unwittingly her gesture heralded an era when flowers became a worldwide expression of communication. The great age of commercial carnation growing, then in its infancy, was ready to expand beyond anyone's imagination. In the 20th century, carnations became one of the most widely recognized flowers and one of the varieties most often used by contemporary florists in their wedding bouquets and funeral wreaths. Bizarres and flakes might have passed into history, but new cultivars, new perceptions of the perfect bloom, were ready to take their place.

factories, many of the flower varieties they had bred faded away. There was increasing criticism that over-emphasis on flowers at the expense of general plant health had debilitated carnations. Inevitably there was a decline in their popularity.

By the end of World War I bizarres and flakes had all but disappeared from the scene. Imagine the disappointment of London schoolmaster and carnation enthusiast Thomas Hogg, had he witnessed their demise. In his book on carnations, written in 1820, he listed nearly 400 varieties of flakes and bizarres.

Not everyone despaired of the genus, however. On the occasion of the first official Mother's Day service in the U.S.A., in May 1908, Miss Anna Jarvis sent 500 white carnations to the Methodist

Below: Rich, velvety red is always a seductive color for dianthus lovers.

CHAPTER 3

The Progenitors: Dianthus Species

The species *Dianthus* were introduced to England from their native European or Asian habitats. Later, they traveled from there to North America and other countries of the New World with the early colonists, but because many species are closely related and identification therefore problematical, they are difficult to find. Catalogs from time to time describe selected species, available either as seeds or plants, but there is no guarantee that the naming of these is totally reliable. Unlike heritage rose enthusiasts or specialist iris growers, few gardeners seek *Dianthus* species for their collections. Their importance lies rather in the genes they have bequeathed to today's plants. By knowing the parentage of any particular cultivar, gardeners then have some understanding of what characteristics to expect when they grow it.

Above: A simple, uncomplicated old pink.
Opposite: Always popular, *Dianthus deltoides* makes a vibrant combination with cornflowers.

Most of those we can find are hardy perennials and some will produce flowers for a long season. As with many species, the flowers tend to be less complex than those of hybrids that breeders have created. They possess a simple beauty, timeless in its appeal. The flowers have usually only five petals, often with serrated edges; the color patterns are uncomplicated, either one clear color or showing a central eye or zone of a contrasting color.

The species

In general, *Dianthus* enjoy warm summers and dislike humidity. They also prefer a site with full sun and a well-drained soil. Refer to Chapter 5, Cultivation of Dianthus (page 45) for more details on their care. Where the preferences of species differ from this norm, details are given with the description of the species below.

Dianthus alpinus (zones 3–9). A native of the European Alps where it grows among limestone

A dainty, white-flowered form of *Dianthus arenarius* with green, grass-like foliage, thrives in a container.

rocks, this was introduced into England around 1759 and is one of the early-blooming species. It has a dwarf, compact habit and the flowers—large, clear pink in color with crimson spots and a central eye—are borne on short stems. Foliage is dark green and is often covered by the mass of flowers. This species has been extensively used by breeders, the best-known cultivars being those of the Allwoodii alpinus group, dating from the 1920s. The plants range in height up to 10 in (25 cm) and produce mainly double flowers, in shades of pink, starting from early summer.

Dianthus arenarius (zones 3–8), often called the sand pink, originated in mountainous regions of Europe. It has small, fragrant, green-tinged white flowers with fringed edges, on stems up to 9 in (23 cm). Unlike other *Dianthus* species, the flowers stand well above the tuft-forming plants that grow only about 4 in (10 cm) high. As its name implies, this pink thrives in sandy soil and is a great plant for a rock garden.

Dianthus armeria (zones 4–8) originated in Europe and was mentioned in a text by the 16th-century herbalist Gerard. Also known as the Deptford pink,

this species was introduced into England in the middle of the 18th century, where it now grows wild on dry banks, stony, sandy slopes and hilly pastures. In Kentucky and as far north as Quebec and Ontario, it is found on roadsides and in fields. Growing to about 16 in (40 cm) high and wide, the plant bears small, deep-rose flowers with petals that are diamond-shaped with blunt-ended points on diamond-shaped petals. As can be guessed from its wild habits, it is easy to cultivate.

Dianthus arvernensis (syn *D. monspessularius*, zone 4). This compact, cushion plant comes from the Auvergne Mountains in central France. Easy to grow, it flowers prolifically, covering itself with a mass of sweetly perfumed rose-pink blooms. The 6-in (15-cm) stems are short and stiff. The cultivar 'Camla' has flowers of a deeper color on a plant even more compact at 4 in (10 cm).

Dianthus barbatus (zones 3–9) is the original sweet William known in England since at least 1573, and subsequently taken to North America where it is now a popular plant in summer gardens. A large color range of modern hybrids is available. (See also page 40.)

Dianthus caryophyllus (zones 5–9) is widely believed to be the sole species in the development of the border carnation, though few gardeners would recognize its original form in the full-petaled, double carnation flowers of many hues that we know today. In fact, its genes are found in most hybrids across the range of carnations and pinks. It's a tall plant that can reach a height of 24 in (60 cm) with blue-gray, glaucous foliage. The flower is single, bright magenta-pink in color, with only five petals.

Sometimes called the "divine flower," this species is also known as the "wild carnation" or "clove pink." Although its exact origins are obscure, it is a native of Europe and grows there on rocks and

Above left: Brilliant *Dianthus deltoides*.
Above right: *Dianthus deltoides* 'Alba'

wall ruins. A romantic aura clings to it. Is it the perfume? Or is it the fact that any plant that will find a foothold in gray stone walls must do so for love?

The clove pink was once used in syrups, cordials and conserves, and was prescribed in traditional European herbal medicine for coronary and nervous disorders. The flowers, steeped in white wine, were also used as culinary flavorings and were even thought to be an aphrodisiac. If you can find this plant, try adding the flowers to distilled vinegar for a delicate, herbal, clove-like taste (from *The Illustrated Herb Encyclopedia* by Kathi Keville (Michael Friedman, 1991).

Dianthus chinensis (syn *D. sinensis*, zones 7–10), known as the "Chinese pink" or "Indian pink," is another important ancestor of many of the garden varieties of carnations and pinks that we grow today. It comes from the hills and mountains of eastern Asia. Its flowers are sweetly scented, rose-red with a purple eye. Classified as an annual in colder zones, it will grow as a short-lived perennial where climate allows. Its height varies from 6–28 in

(15–70 cm). *D. chinensis* 'Heddewigii' is a popular cultivar that grows 8–10 in (20–25 cm) high and bears lots of large, fringed flowers in various colors.

Dianthus deltoides (zones 3–10). Often called the "maiden pink" because each stem carries only one flower, this is a vigorous, free-flowering plant through early summer. It naturalizes easily, which it has done in New England, where it now grows wild. Each plant forms a mat of bright green foliage up to 3 ft (1 m) across—ideal for planting on slopes. One of the few dianthus to thrive in partial shade, its blooms are tiny and bright pink with more deeply colored markings in the center, though there are also red, paler pink and white forms. These and its many hybrids are bright, attractive garden plants. Their flowers seem to glow, especially in evening light or in a shaded corner. As a bonus, they're easy to grow and self-seed readily. Great for ground cover or growing in cracks in paving.

Popular *Dianthus deltoides* cultivars include:
'Albus', dwarf form, 4 in (10 cm) high, abundant, single, white flowers in early summer.

The slightly taller 'Zing Rose', bright, strong, rose pink with darker ring around the eye of the flower. Flowers prolifically from early summer, and if sheared off, will continue flowering until the first frost. Low-growing mat 6 in (15 cm) high.

'Brilliant', is a dwarf form with bright crimson flowers.

'Major Sterne', has bronze foliage and carmine flowers.

'Flashing Light', 6–8 in (15–20 cm) high, scarlet flowers and dark foliage on dwarf, tufted plants.

'Microchips', a mat-forming plant, produces small red flowers with bright eyes; blooms three months from sowing.

'Arctic Fire', white flowers with glowing red eye, 7 in (18 cm) high.

'Erectus', bushy plants, red flowers in early to midsummer.

'Shrimp', spreading habit, with flowers of salmon-pink.

Canta Libra Mixed is a strain with bronze foliage and pink, white and red flowers 6–8 in (15–20 cm).

Dianthus erinaceus (zones 4–9). This is a dwarf alpine plant, native to mountains in the Middle East and sometimes known as the hedgehog pink. Forming wide-spreading but low, prickly cushions, 2–4 in (6–10 cm) high and bearing solitary, minute, fringed rose-red flowers, it is an ideal plant for troughs or rock gardens in hot, dry areas.

Dianthus gratianopolitanus (syn D. caesius)

Dianthus gratianopolitanus syn ***D. caesius*** (zones 3–8). Once this was called the "mountain pink," but now it is widely known as the "Cheddar pink," named after the district in England where it long ago naturalized and grows wild on limestone rocks. With flowers single, tooth-petaled and sweetly scented, it grows 4–6 in (10–15 cm) tall and has been used extensively in the breeding of cultivars that are low-growing and suitable for rock and scree gardens.

Cultivars of *Dianthus gratianopolitanus* include:

'Grandiflorus', a mat-forming plant with pink flowers on 6-in (15-cm) stems.

'Bath's Pink', which is more heat-tolerant than most pinks and therefore a good plant for humid areas, makes a cushion to 12 in (30 cm) and bears in summer small, pink, fringed flowers with maroon centers.

'Lace Hero' has semi-double summer flowers in white with plum-colored centers. Foliage is gray.

'Tiny Rubies' forms a compact clump of green foliage with tiny, deep pink, single to double flowers held on slender stems well above the foliage in early summer. A plant for the lover of miniature flowers.

'Spottii' has rose-red flowers, splashed with silver.

Dianthus knappii (zones 3–8) has yellow flowers. It is found in parts of Italy, the former Yugoslavia, Hungary and Romania, where it grows in grassy places and scrub. Rarely seen in gardens, it is a rather untidy plant of variable height, according to climate, and its coloring has been elusive in breeders' efforts to introduce yellow into garden pinks. Small flowers appear in clusters on stems to 15 in (40 cm) throughout summer. A selected form called 'Yellow Harmony' is available as seed, as is *D. knappii* 'Yellow Beauty'.

Dianthus myrtinervius (zones 4–8) is another mountain plant, from Macedonia. This species forms dense mats with small, bright green leaves

Dianthus knappii

and single, dark pink flowers with light eyes, only $^1/_2$ in (1 cm) across. Plant this one in a rock or scree garden, but as it grows only about 3 in (8 cm) high, make sure it is not overwhelmed by taller, more aggressive plants. Keep it trimmed.

Dianthus neglectus (zone 4) comes from the Swiss and Italian Alps, so is well suited to winter snows. The leaves are narrow, like grass, glaucous and only reach about 2 in (5 cm) high—totally overwhelmed by the quite large flowers that grow on 4-in (10-cm) stems. Colors vary from palest pink through rose to carmine and petals have a buff reverse.

Dianthus plumarius (zones 3–9). Southern Russia is the original home of this species and its genes are present in most of the garden pinks we grow today. Those with strong traits from *D. plumarius* are variously called "cottage pinks," "spice pinks" or "grass pinks." The species was supposedly introduced to England about 1629 and has always been cherished for its sweet perfume and abundant flowering, from spring to fall. A good plant for warmer areas, its petals are deeply fringed in a pale lilac-pink color.

Popular cultivars of *Dianthus plumarius* include:

'Cyclops', with single flowers in shades of white, red or rose, blooming from late spring right through to fall on 12-in (30-cm) stems.

'Spooky', a bi-color with rose centers and white edges and deeply fringed petals.

'Pheasant's Eye', with single blooms.

'Superbus Prima Donna', a taller plant with big flowers that are good for cutting.

Sonata Double Mix is a strain that gives double flowers in a varied mix of colors, also useful for cutting.

Dianthus superbus (zones 3–8). This is the fringed pink described by herbalist John Gerard in 1596 as the "spotted sweet John." Parkinson, in his *Herbal* published about 30 years later, calls it the "Feathered Pinke of Austria." Widespread in its native habitat, extending from France and the Netherlands east to Russia and Siberia, and south to Japan and Taiwan. The conditions it likes are almost as varied as the countries of origin. One of the few dianthus that will tolerate continual moisture, it is found in damp, grassy places, on dunes, in open woods and in mountain meadows. The flowers are pale to deep, lilac pink, single and deeply fringed. Those florists of old who strove for rounded flowers must have hated it.

The form of the species flowers has contributed to the feathery petals of the modern hybrids, known as the Rainbow Loveliness strain. These were raised, before 1926, by Montagu Allwood, probably the

best-known dianthus breeder of last century and the flamboyant founding partner of the carnation specialist firm, Allwood Bros., in the U.K. This strain is very fragrant, another trait inherited from the species, and has recently found wide popularity in North America. The blooms, produced on 18-in (45-cm) stems from late spring until midsummer, are so finely cut they resemble frilly pinwheels. Colors range from white to pale lilac, to plum and reddish violet. They are easily raised from seed, marginally perennial and hardy to zone 5.

'White Loveliness', presumed to be a hybrid of the species, was raised by Allwood in 1928 and has white blooms.

Above left: 'Emile Paré', which will tolerate some shade, grows happily with perennial geraniums.
Above right: Complementary pinks.

Dianthus superbus is said to have been a favorite of Linnaeus, hence its name. According to *The Encyclopedia of Medicinal Plants* (Dorling Kindersley, 1996), this dianthus is cultivated in the eastern provinces of China and gathered in summer and autumn, when it is in flower, for use in traditional medicine to treat kidney and urinary problems. *D. superbus* or *qu mai* was first mentioned in the Chinese herbal known as the *Divine Husbandman's Classic*, written in the first century AD.

CHAPTER 4

Dianthus for Today's Gardeners

Pinks

The time-honored name "pink," embracing a wide range of mostly perfumed dianthus that look like miniature carnations, is really rather misleading. 'Mrs. Sinkins', who has been around since the 19th century, must feel quite excluded, as she is very well known and is decidedly white.

There are several explanations of the derivation of the name pink. Some say it comes from the old Dutch word *pinkster*, meaning Whitsuntide or Pentecost, a religious date in the Christian calendar, when pinks would have been used in floral decorations. Some say it refers to the central "eye," a feature of old pinks. Certainly, the French name for carnation, *oeillet*, means "little eye." But "pinking," or scalloped edges, were in fashion on clothes in Elizabethan times and this seems a good enough reason to assume that pink describes the serrated edges of its petals. The name of the plant, in turn, lent itself to the name of the color and so a new term entered the English language.

In fact, dianthus colors range from white through palest pink, mauve and salmon, to rich, velvety crimson. They might be **selfs** (one solid color); **laced** (a background color etched with a contrasting color just inside the petal edge that repeats the color in the center of the bloom), or **one color with a contrasting "eye."** They may bear single or double flowers and have petals that are deeply fringed, serrated, or rounded and almost completely smooth.

The predominant ancestor of garden pinks is *Dianthus plumarius*, although D. *sinensis*, D. *caryophyllus* and D. *gratianopolitanus* also feature in the

'Isobel', a modern laced variety.

family tree of many hybrids. The descriptive adjective *plumarius* refers to the serrated petal edging and this species determines the generally compact, bushy habit that makes these tidy plants for borders and edgings.

They have evolved over many centuries, hybridizing sometimes intentionally and often by happenstance, for they're promiscuous plants and cross-fertilize freely without human intervention.

Pinks tend to be hardier than carnations and are tolerant of pollution. They vary in height from tiny rock-garden plants that make prickly-looking hummocks only a few inches (several centimeters) high

Above: 'Crimson Ace', a pink dating from the 1960s that is still popular.

Above: A 19th-century pink, 'Earl of Essex', tends to split its calyx, but it is loved for its perfume.

to sprawling cultivars with flowers on long stems up to 12 in (30 cm) tall that make excellent cut flowers.

The following descriptions will help you know what characteristics to look for when choosing pinks for your garden.

Old-fashioned pinks

Initially regarded as the country cousins of the more sophisticated carnations, pinks came into vogue as florists' flowers about 1770 and the true old-fashioned varieties, those cultivated pre-19th century, are generally believed to have only one ancestor, the species *Dianthus plumarius*. However, such a narrow classification serves little practical purpose today.

Many breeders believe border carnations (*Dianthus caryophyllus*) entered the family tree in the 19th century. 'Mrs. Sinkins', bred in the 1860s, resulted supposedly from crossing 'Old Fringed White', a direct descendant from *D. plumarius*, with an old clove carnation (or border carnation). She is definitely called an old-fashioned pink, as are other varieties from long ago, including 'Inchmery', first grown in the 18th century, and 'Paddington', introduced in 1830, but the group also includes those with an old-fashioned habit—strong sweet perfume, a single seasonal flowering and low, clumping growth.

These perennial varieties flower briefly in late spring or early summer for two to three weeks of perfumed glory. Their flowers are small, borne on stems that are never very long; they may be single or double and their petals are serrated or fringed. Flowering may be profuse or sparse. Where several varieties are planted close together, they will breed. The result is a spreading clump, with flowers that complement each other in color and size and make an eye-catching show for several weeks. And the perfume is delicious.

The old-fashioned pinks are not long-lived plants. They tend to become straggly after about three years and produce fewer blooms. If they're precious, take cuttings to avoid losing them.

Above and left: Typical of the confusion in naming pinks, both these varieties are known as 'Charles Musgrave'.

Gardeners with a liking for nostalgia cherish the idea that some of these pinks are thought to go back as far as the 17th century, but naming of garden pinks is a notoriously fickle affair. Some old cultivars die out, a similar one may be bred years later and the old name adopted. John Galbally talks about his research in this area. He relates that a famous English breeder advertised for propagating material of the true 'Mrs. Sinkins', always regarded as a white flower. Of the 50 samples he received, no two were identical. When Galbally investigated further, he found that the original 'Mrs. Sinkins', introduced in 1868, in fact used to have a splash of crimson on its petals. He raised seedlings from a clone he believed to be genuine and produced a range of progeny, including some that displayed a crimson eye.

Painted ladies are now regarded as old pinks. They date from the 17th century and have single flowers, a white background and regular patterns "painted" in shades of red or pink on the petals. Similar at first glance to laced pinks, they differ from these in the breadth of the colored markings. 'Constance Finnis' is a modern painted lady.

A product of the mid-19th century, and rarely seen nowadays, are "mule pinks." They resulted from a cross between *Dianthus barbatus* and *D. plumarius*. As their name implies, they are sterile and had to be propagated by cuttings. The only one

Above: 'Emile Paré'—notice the typical bright green foliage at the upper edge.
Right: The original 'Mrs Sinkins' displayed the cerise markings of this flower.

still available is 'Emile Paré', bred in 1840 and recognizable by its bright green foliage, evidence of its *D. barbatus* parentage. Old pinks (and some modern cultivars)—those that flower only once each season—should not be pinched (see page 48), and because their season is restricted, include with them in the garden some newer varieties that repeat flower but which are also scented.

Popular varieties include:

'Charles Musgrave' syn 'Musgrave's Pink', a neat, compact plant that flowers profusely, its clean, white, single blooms each having a clear green eye.

'Inchmery', an old-fashioned favorite has clove-scented, delicate, pale pink blooms that flourish over a long season.

'Bat's Double Red' a free-flowering variety dating from the 18th century. The fringed, semi-double and strawberry-red blooms have darker markings at the center.

'Rose de Mai' has deep pink, very double flowers and a heavenly perfume. Plants form a low-growing mat with a tendency to spread.

Laced pinks

The earliest "laced pinks," also perennials, date back to the 18th century. From their first appearance, these precisely marked flowers were an instant hit.

In 1772 James Major, an English gardener, noticed an unusual flower among a batch of seedling pinks he had grown from seed collected the previous year. Its edges were threaded with the same dark color that decorated the center of the flower. He refused an enormous offer of ten guineas for the plant, named it 'Duchess of Ancaster' after his employer, and propagated as many as he could, subsequently selling them for a great profit. This was the beginning of a cult that lasted well into the 19th century.

By 1792 a nurseryman's catalog listed 99 varieties. Pinks, which until then had occupied a low status in the carnation hierarchy, were sought after by florists. No longer considered fit only to plant at

A modern laced pink showing how variations may commonly occur on a single plant.

the front of a border or to use in posies, they were the focus of breeders vying with each other to produce ever more perfect, laced blooms. Through the upsets of the Napoleonic Wars and economic restructuring caused by the introduction of income tax, pinks maintained their popularity as collectors' plants. Unlike tulips, which at one time might have cost anything up to 1000 pounds, pinks were always affordable.

Growers in London, Lancaster and, above all, the florist-weavers in Paisley, Scotland, adopted these delicately signatured flowers as their specialty. They competed fiercely at shows and quarreled about standards. Initially, the background had to be pure white, but by the early 19th century pink had appeared as a base color. Petals were fringed or serrated and laced with shades of crimson to purple—

Above left: *Salvia superba* 'Mainacht' with a modern laced dianthus.
Above right: 'Kiwi Magic'

until the Paisley weavers aimed to eliminate the ancestral serrations of *Dianthus plumarius* and developed rounded or smooth edges to the petals. Most valued was a white flower, smoothly finished, with a center so darkly red as to appear almost black and a border of the same color.

Differences arose between aficionados in the north and those in the south. Northern growers despised the full-petaled, "bursting" pinks. They called them "London mops" and criticized their "mongrel lacing." They favored "whole blowers," with fewer petals that did not burst their calyxes. Southerners, in their turn, scorned winning blooms with as few as eight petals.

Market forces have not changed with the ages. It was demand from the competitive florists that drove sales. They constantly desired new varieties to exhibit, and much-vaunted cultivars appeared in catalogs only to be replaced with surprising speed. Thomas Hogg, in the first decades of the 19th century, listed over 150 named pinks in his third *Trea-*

tise. Some of the names were scarcely a marketer's dream—'Beauty of Ugliness' was one; 'Hopkin's Scarecrow' another. When the shows declined, the supply of laced pinks dried up. By the end of the 19th century they were hard to find in catalogs.

There are, however, modern varieties of laced pinks. 'Dad's Favourite' appeared in 1932 and is still to be found. James Douglas, an English flower breeder, produced laced pinks before World War II, but these were less enduring than those bred in the 1950s by a barrister in London, F. R. McQuown. He bred laced pinks as a hobby and several of his cultivars were sold commercially with the prefix "London" in their names. 'London Brocade' was used by John Galbally as a breeding parent and from it he produced the highly successful and popular 'Becky Robinson', clove-scented and laced in ruby red. The flower has an instant charm, though it tends to sprawl in favorable growing conditions, as do several varieties from other breeding lines.

Laced pinks vary in height from 9 to 14 in (23 to 35 cm). They bloom from early to midsummer, with a few varieties continuing on into fall. The lacing can vary from season to season and according to growing conditions.

Popular cultivars include: 'Painted Beauty', with fragrant, fringed blooms, blush pink and overlaid with a wine-red pattern, appearing in early summer on stems 6–8 in (15–20 cm) long, above a broad mat of grassy, gray-green leaves. This plant tolerates southern heat and humidity better than most dianthus, provided drainage is good. 'Dad's Favourite', also called 'A.J. Macself' after the man who more than 60 years ago discovered it growing in an old garden, has flowers that are fully double and shapely, white with a distinctive ruby-red lacing. It blooms late in the season and continues in flower for a long time.

Above: Unusually shaded 'Devon Magic' blooms on a slender stem and has fine foliage.

Modern pinks

Under this heading we have included perennial pinks raised by various breeders in the 20th century. Many of these, with a rounded, more symmetrical flower form, include show pinks. As with all types of carnations, cultivars tend to be ephemeral. A star is born, praised and sought after for a time, but inevitably a bright new star appears over the horizon, the old fades from view and the new takes its place briefly.

Some modern pinks, which produce large, double flowers on tall stems, and are useful as cut flowers, can be difficult to distinguish from border carnations. Flowering times vary, according to their breeding lines, but many are repeat flowering and provide several flushes from early summer to mid-fall. "Selfs" refer to blooms that are all one color; "bi-colors" show two colors in contrasting rings; "laced pinks" are as described above, and "fancies" refer to all the other color combinations.

These plants need to be "stopped," or pinched back to encourage a bushy habit and prolific blooming. They make substantial clumps in a garden setting. With their often-heady perfume and wide range of colors, the flowers appeal to both traditional and innovative gardeners.

The pinks that have had the greatest influence on modern garden varieties are those which bear

Above: 'Monica Wyatt', early-flowering and perfumed.

the name of their hybridizer, Montagu Allwood. In 1910 he crossed 'Old Fringed', a semi-double, white, garden pink with a perpetual-flowering carnation, thus introducing the repeat-flowering, or remontant, habit into the old pinks, which had formerly flowered only once in a season. The offspring from

Above: 'Doris' is an old favorite.
Right: 'Haytor White'
Bottom right: 'Letitia Wyatt'

this cross were named *Dianthus allwoodii* and they appear in the family tree of most cultivars bred throughout the rest of the 20th century. Best-known and most enduring of Allwood's pinks is 'Doris', loved by gardeners around the world for its bushy, clumping habit and long-stemmed, delicate shell-pink blooms splashed in the center with terra cotta. Both its style and fragrance make 'Doris' an excellent plant for cut flowers.

British breeder C. H. Herbert, who was active in the first 30 years of the 20th century, produced cultivars with non-splitting calyxes, among them one called 'Bridesmaid'—pale pink with a scarlet center—later superseded in popularity by 'Doris'. 'Bridesmaid' remained an important cultivar for subsequent breeders, however, and Herbert's pinks crossed with *Dianthus allwoodii* gave birth to the Imperial Pinks, of which 'Crimson Ace' and 'Iceberg' continue to be grown.

Another breeder's name that appears in several attractive varieties currently available is that of Cecil Wyatt, also an Englishman. Produced in the 1970s, many of his cultivars have starred in exhibits at the Chelsea Flower Show. 'Haytor White' boasts a lovely, clean, slightly serrated flower, though the plant has a rather sprawling habit. 'Monica Wyatt' and her sisters 'Valda', 'Anne' and 'Letitia' are all attractive flowers, good for cutting.

The Devon Series of pinks comes from H. R. Whetman and Son, and several have received awards from the Royal Horticultural Society in Britain.

More recently, New Zealand breeder and co-author of this book, Dr. Keith Hammett, has produced some interesting hybrids. He planted laced pink seed from John Galbally in England and from the seedlings selected the original and highly successful Kiwi Series. He then began crossing his Kiwi Series with the best garden pinks that had stood the test of time. The first seedling that came from an early cross produced little single, pink flowers, not at all what Keith was looking for. However, at summer's end it was still flowering bravely and after trials, when it proved a good performer, Keith named it 'Far Cry' because it was a long way from that which he had been seeking. It proved to be an important parent, imparting its repeat flowering characteristic to its offspring, and is sold as 'Baby Blanket' in the United States.

Subsequently, Keith bred a range of cultivars, including doubles, which all repeat flower and make good garden subjects. Of these, the following cultivars are popular: 'Counterpart', 'Speckled Dale', 'Pink Spray', 'Royal Velvet' and 'Sidekick'.

As new hybrids are released, lists in catalogs change and names often disappear. The following three Allwoodii hybrids are mentioned as examples of plants that have met with wide approval and have lasted in catalog lists: 'Helen', with fragrant, deep pink flowers and compact growth; 'Ian', released in 1938, free-flowering with deep crimson

'Checkmate'

blooms; and 'Alice', well scented and bearing ivory-white flowers with a crimson eye.

Also popular as garden plants in North America are the many *Dianthus deltoides* hybrids available. They are easy to grow and form dainty plants with slender stems, each bearing one bloom. Hybrid details appear under the description of the species commencing on page 23.

Rock-garden pinks

Rock gardens are frequently home to species *Dianthus*, often called alpines, though not all of them originated in the high alpine regions. These are not spectacular plants. They don't cry out for attention. They won't bowl you over with masses of

Above left: A cushion-forming cultivar that echoes the habit of some species—excellent for those who love texture.
Above right: Prolific and reliable 'Pikes Pink' is great for rock gardens.

"pickable," perfumed blooms. But they are intriguing. They have texture and form. Presenting as often tightly compact, neat little gray hedgehogs of plants that look good all year and bear bright, highly perfumed flowers in spring and summer, they are excellent for containers and look superb in rough, concrete-type planters or even old stone sinks. And they are hardy, growing well in zones 4 to 8, with many surviving in zone 3.

In their natural habitat these species pinks flourish in the cracks and crevices of limestone mountains where pockets of loose gravel and stones keep their roots cool and ensure free drainage, so they won't need well-fertilized soil rich in humus to keep them happy.

Growing taller than the ground-hugging *Dianthus microlepis* or *D. arenarius*, but still neat in habit, are hybrids derived from *D. alpinus* or introductions from the cross-breeding of *D. allwoodii* with *D. alpinus*, *D. gratianopolitanus* and *D. arenarius*. A group of heavily flowering, dwarf plants called Whatfield pinks are also suitable for rock gardens. Hybridized by Joan Schofield in England, they are the offspring of alpine hybrids crossed with *D. deltoides*, *D. neglectus* and *D. erinaceus*.

More recently, Keith Hammett has added to the range of plants suitable for rock gardens with 'Pink Spray', 'Side Kick', 'Counterpart' and 'Baby Blanket' (syn 'Far Cry'). In addition, his 'Far North' (white single), 'Royal Velvet' (deep crimson splashed with white), 'Far Pink' (a darker pink version of 'Far Cry'), 'Shrewsbury' and the just-named 'Small Talk' can be recommended for use in the rock garden.

These modern cultivars require more feeding than the species; planting pockets should contain at least 4 in (10 cm) of soil that includes plant food. Mulching with pebbles, preferably limestone, will help to keep the roots cool in summer.

Other cultivars for the rock garden include 'Sweet Wivelsfield', a hybrid that produces large trusses of flowers in a range of colors, each with the center of the flower a darker shade. It's a bushy plant growing to about 12 in (30 cm) high. 'Pikes Pink', a strong, compact plant with pale pink, scented, double blooms, is an enduring cultivar that flowers from early to midsummer (height 3 in (7.5 cm)). 'Mars' is a smaller, ground-hugging, clumping plant with blue-gray foliage and large, bright crimson, clove-scented blooms. It needs perfect drainage, full sun and free air circulation—don't let weeds or other more vigorous plants overpower it. 'Inshriach Dazzler' has single flowers, carmine pink with buff undersides. 'Waithman's Beauty' is scented and bears flowers of ruby-red flecked with white. An excellent plant for growing in a windowbox or rockery, it is neat, has an upright habit and blooms profusely throughout summer. 'Joan's Blood' is a hybrid from *D. alpinus*. It has deep red flowers with a darker center carried on 2-in (5-cm) stems.

Some strains available as seeds: *Dianthus gratianopolitanus* Mixed Colors, called Cheddar pinks, give a selection of single, fragrant, pink, red and white flowers; Rock Garden Blend is a selection of seed made up from a wide mix of species and varieties; Rondo Mix is a selection with mixed-color blooms on short plants growing to 6 in (15 cm) that are not hardy and are grown as annuals; *D. allwoodii* 'Alpinus Mixed' produces early-summer flowers in many shades of pink on plants that are about 8 in (20 cm) tall.

Dianthus for summer beds

Called variously Indian pinks, China pinks, annual pinks or rainbow pinks, these are showy, low-growing (12–15 in/30–45 cm), clump-forming plants that smother themselves all summer in short-stemmed, brightly colored flowerheads up to 2 in (5 cm) in diameter. Most cultivars are derived from the species *Dianthus sinensis* crossed with *D. barbatus* (sweet William). *Dianthus sinensis* (syn *D. chinensis*) is a native of China and North India, and Western gardeners have known of this plant since about 1705 when seed was sent from China to Paris by a French missionary. Soon popular in Parisian gardens, this dianthus crossed the Channel and by the next decade was found growing in English gardens. As with other dianthus, they crossed the Atlantic with the early English colonists.

Often sold by color, these plants are good for bedding schemes, containers, borders or rock gardens, and resemble sweet William, with slightly larger flowers arranged in smaller bunches. They can be bought as seeds, sown under warm cover in winter, and the seedlings planted outdoors once all danger of frost has passed. They take 20 weeks from planting to flower. Alternatively, buy them as small potted plants in spring if you are looking for instant color.

In some areas grasshoppers can be a problem for these plants and good air circulation is necessary to prevent crown rot—take care if you are tempted to mulch around these dianthus in summer. Where soils tend to retain moisture, plant them in raised beds.

Bred by Keith Hammett, 'Royal Velvet' is attractive in rock gardens and small containers.

Color co-ordinated: annual dianthus 'Strawberry Parfait' and ornamental oregano.

Usually treated as annuals, they are often regarded as biennials or short-lived perennials in mild climates (zones 8–10) and, cut back in autumn, they will survive to produce a second season of prolific flowering in the next summer. Use them in containers to make attractive displays combined with other low-growing bright annuals or perennials—great for adding color around a pool or on the patio.

Some of these cultivars, such as the Telstar Series, are heat tolerant and in the warmer southeastern states can be used as a cool-season bedding plant for color over winter. Plant them from November to the beginning of March and they will provide several months of pleasure before they need replacing by late May.

Popular strains include: carpet hybrids that come in crimson, salmon, scarlet and shades of rose, flower early and produce clumps 6–8 in (15–20 cm) high; Charms (or Magic Charms)—hybrids in mixed colors, producing clusters of fringed flowers in clumps 6 in (15 cm) high; the hardy and heat-tolerant Ideal hybrids in a mix of colors with single, serrated flowers, forming clumps 8–10 in (20–25 cm) high; Princess hybrids with large, fringed, red, salmon or white flowers growing 6–8 in (15–20 cm) high.

Specific cultivars worth seeking out include: 'Flash Pink', which flowers early, is heat tolerant and clumps to 12 in (30 cm); 'Raspberry Parfait' bears deep red, fringed flowers with a pale eye and grows 8–10 in (20–25 cm) high; 'Strawberry Parfait' has bicolored, fringed flowers with a reddish eye and pale pink outer rim and it grows 8–10 in (20–25 cm) high; 'Snowfire' produces fringed, white flowers with red centers and grows 6–8 in (15–20 cm) high.

Sweet William
Known botanically as *Dianthus barbatus* (for their flowers with bearded throats), these plants bloom from spring through summer. They grow 12–24 in

(30–60 cm) high and bear densely packed, slightly flattened heads of single or double flowers in myriad shades of pink, red, mauve, purple and white, some with auricula-type "eyes." All of them are good as cut flowers. Their foliage differs from most other dianthus; it lacks the waxy texture and gray-blue tones usually associated with carnations and is composed of often-bright green rosettes of lance-shaped leaves.

One popular cultivar, *Dianthus barbatus* 'Nigricans' (or 'Sooty'), is an exciting shade of red, so dark as to appear almost black in some light, and its foliage is likewise a dark, sooty red-green.

Thought to be a survivor from the 17th century is *Dianthus barbatus magnificum*, also known as 'King Willie'. Its foliage is bronze, its double flowers dark crimson and it grows to only about 6 in (15 cm) high. Difficult to find and difficult to keep, take cuttings every year if you are lucky enough to have it in your garden.

The bright colors and spicy perfume of sweet Williams have made them a favorite in cottage gar-

Above: Dark-flowered sweet William is an unusual combination with an orange helianthemum.

dens for centuries. Possibly introduced into England in the 12th century by Carthusian monks, they were used extensively in 1533 at Hampton Court when Henry VIII had some landscaping done—though few would have called his a cottage garden.

Gerard describes the pleasant white flowers, spotted with red, found in London gardens. He comments that, "These plants are kept and maintained in gardens more to please the eye, than either the nose or the belly. These plants are not used either in meat or medicine, but esteemed for their beauty to decke up gardens, the bosomes of the beautifull, garlands and crownes for pleasure."

Why sweet William? Some believe William the Conqueror is celebrated in their name; others credit the fame to William Shakespeare. A stronger thread of opinion favors William Augustus, Duke of Cumberland and conqueror of the Scots at the battle of Culloden in the 18th century. Given, however, that Gerard refers to them as 'Sweet-Williams' in 1597, the latter opinion can scarcely be valid.

Above: Auricula-eyed sweet William.

William Cobbett, never suggested as the progenitor of their name, but one-time British politician, sometime pioneer in the United States and garden advisor extraordinaire writes about them in *The English Gardener* (1829):

This plant is too well known to need any particular description; it is biennial or triennial, but is usually grown as a biennial, the seed being sown one year to blow [bloom] the next. It is one of the most ornamental plants of the garden, an oblong bed of sweet-williams being, to my eye, the most beautiful thing that one can behold of the flower kind. The varieties of color are without end, and the stiff stalk of the plants holds them up to view in so complete a manner that there is nothing left to wish for in this plant.

While a modern gardener's opinion may differ from William Cobbett's on their arrangement in the garden, few would dispute that, as a super-bright display in summer, sweet William is dazzling. Once you have these plants in your garden, you will have them forever, as they self-seed with abandon. They are very adaptable and will tolerate some shade. Most will grow in zones 3–9.

Popular strains include: Double Midget Mixed, which produces double flowers in a variety of colors on plants that bloom at 6 in (15 cm) tall; Single Midget Mixed are slightly smaller than the above, with very dense flowerheads and are great for rock gardens; Hollandia Mix will bloom five months from seed and grow to 24 in (60 cm) tall; Super Duplex Double Choice Mixed grows extra-large, double, brightly colored flowers on 18-in (45-cm) plants; 'Holborn Glory' has crimson and white flowers on 24-in (60-cm) plants; 'Homeland' produces flowers that are dark red with white centers on plants 24 in (60 cm) tall; 'Newport Pink' has salmon-pink flowers on 24-in (60-cm) plants; 'Nigricans' produces stunning, dark, red-black flowers on 24-in (60-cm) plants, its foliage dark bronze-green; 'Scarlet Beauty'—not hard to guess the color

of these—they also grow to 24 in (60 cm); and 'White' has extra large flowers on 24-in (60-cm) plants.

Annual carnations

Less common than the above varieties in some countries but popular in North America, annual or seed carnations look like the flowers you buy in a florist shop. The plants grow to about 18 in (45 cm), the stems are not long and the flowers have a wonderful perfume. The blooms are smaller than those of border carnations and the petals more crowded, with serrated edges, rather than the rounded blooms of the border varieties. Available in shades of pink, red, salmon, white and yellow, the flowers are great for picking, though their buds don't open in water. Newly opened flowers will last five days.

These plants are hybrids, descended from *Dianthus chinensis* and *D. caryophyllus*. The best known are the Grenadin strains and the Chabauds; the latter, named after a French professor of botany, are an improved form of the Marguerite carnation, believed to have originated in Sicily. The open pollinated dwarf varieties of annual carnations are a mixed bag, both for color and flower form.

Designated annuals, these carnations are not fully hardy in the colder areas of North America, though they will frequently last a second season where winters are not too wet or cold (zones 8–10). If the plants are still in good condition in early fall, they are worth saving. In areas of cold winter temperatures (zone 7 and colder), cover them with evergreen branches, straw or coldframe or, alternatively, lift and pot the plants, and allow them to overwinter in a cold greenhouse.

Many annual carnations are suited to container planting and can be grown through winter in pots in a greenhouse. Maintain the temperature no lower than 55°F (13°C), and they will flower under cover.

Strains include: Giant Chabaud, with fringed, double flowers; Grenadins, which have stouter stems and need less staking than Chabauds; Dwarf

'Greytown', a modern border carnation bred by Keith Hammett reflects a color scheme from long ago.

Grenadins, with a wide range of color, growing only 15 in (38 cm); Fragrance, with a bushy habit; plain-edged Enfants-de-France; and Early Dwarf Vienna, growing only 12 in (30 cm) tall.

Popular cultivars include: 'Cardinal' (Grenadin) with bright scarlet flowers in midsummer; the aptly named yellow 'Golden Sun' (Grenadin); 'King of Black' (Grenadin), a very dark red; and 'Peach Delight' with peach-pink blooms on sturdy stems.

Border carnations

Many of the pinks we grow in our gardens today bear a close resemblance to those that we assume our forebears grew generations ago. Not so border carnations. These are plants that have evolved over five centuries by rigorous selection, some believe solely from innumerable seedlings of the species *Dianthus caryophyllus*.

Though this species varies little in nature, careful selection of seedlings in cultivation over generations has introduced innumerable patterns and color combinations, dictated by the whims of grow-

'Peter Wood', a border carnation bred by John Galbally.

ers and exhibitors of the flowers. It is interesting to note, however, the comment of John Galbally, gleaned from his many years of experience as a breeder and grower of carnations, that when carnations are raised from seed, there is always a proportion of single-flowered plants, many of which resemble their unsophisticated ancestor.

Like pinks, border carnations are hardy and evergreen perennials, growing outdoors in contrast to perpetual-flowering carnations that are raised in greenhouses. Their habit is strong—bushy in their second year, up to 24 in (60 cm)—and even taller when grown in pots under glass. Their flowers are the open, multi-petaled shapes that most people associate with carnations. Growing well in zones 5 to 10, border carnations are excellent as cut flowers, they come in fascinating color combinations and, unlike pinks, include yellow in their spectrum. Some of them are strongly clove scented. Blooming can be from late spring to midsummer.

In their first year the plants grow few flowering stems; in subsequent years flowering stems, producing masses of blooms, emerge from numerous side shoots that develop at the base of the plant. It is from these side shoots that layerings or cuttings are made to create new plants to replace the original when it becomes straggly and loses its vigor.

Border carnations must not be pinched (or stopped), otherwise they will not flower the following year.

We wouldn't be human if we weren't slaves to fashion, and the fashion among border carnations has changed dramatically over the years. In the 18th and 19th centuries these flowers were bred, sometimes fanatically, for exhibition purposes and color combinations evolved that appear quite unnatural to our eyes but were sought after by connoisseurs of the times. As already described, flakes, bizarres and picotees were popular, with strict rules dictating what was acceptable on the show bench. Picotees still exist, but today selfs and fancies with varying background colors are more common. (Selfs are of one color, fancies combine two colors and their blends tend to be subtler, though there are still varieties with marked contrasting patterns.)

In contrast to annual carnations, which usually come in strains with a range of colors, border carnations are always marketed as individual named varieties. Some retain the traditional strong clove scent. Generally speaking, they grow taller than pinks, and the double or semi-double flowers, up to 3 in (8 cm) across, have smooth-edged petals and a rounded profile. They are produced on long stems that need staking. Perhaps this is one reason why they are less popular in today's gardens. In the past, thin bamboo stakes were often used, with less than aesthetic appeal. One solution is to plant several of the same variety close together so they can offer some support for each other and in a large clump artificial supports are less obvious. Some gardeners use dried, forked branches that are subtler than perpendicular stakes.

CHAPTER 5

Cultivation of Dianthus

These plants, natives of southern and eastern Europe and Asia, where winters are cold and summers hot, have thrived for centuries in dry, rocky areas of the Mediterranean countries and in mountain meadows as far east as Japan and Taiwan. The dianthus we plant today, descendants of these ancestral plants, enjoy similar conditions. But those hybrids that we grow outdoors are tolerant plants. They're easy to cultivate in varying conditions, provided summers are not too warm and humid and the plants' need for sharp drainage is met.

Choosing a site

The different groups of *Dianthus*, whether they are perennial pinks, border carnations, sweet William or the annual varieties, all crave summer warmth, sun and light. Choose a site where they will not be hidden in shade beneath overhanging trees or tucked in behind bushy shrubs. Evening dampness can encourage fungal disease, so keep them away from fences and other structures that restrict air movement. With plenty of space they remain healthier plants, so make sure they will not be over-crowded by fast-spreading perennials planted too close. Most dianthus are front-of-the-border plants that want to flaunt their bright colors or their delicate markings for everyone to see. And one of the joys of pinks is their delicious perfume. Plant them where it's easy to bend down and savor their fragrance.

Soil

Soils vary considerably in their composition, from extreme acidity to extreme alkalinity, the relative alkalinity or acidity being expressed as the pH value. A pH of 7 is neutral, the level where dianthus are happy, though they will tolerate some variation on either side. A pH reading of 6.5 and lower indi-

Above: 'Devon Dove', long-stemmed and perfumed.

Prolific and healthy, these two varieties of pinks are happy with their roots burrowed in among rocks.

Dianthus like the free-draining, well-aerated qualities of gravelly or rocky soil, their natural habitat, so it makes sense to provide conditions that simulate this as closely as is reasonable. They are not notably fussy plants but they don't like wet feet and will quickly die in heavy, anaerobic clay conditions where drainage is poor. But, if this is the kind of soil you are blessed with, don't despair. It is possible to change it.

Old books talk about burning the clay or adding mortar rubble to it, but these options are open to very few gardeners today. Coarse sand, dolomite and gypsum will help to open up clay; adding quantities of humus is also effective. Rotted leaves, mushroom compost (which contains lime and is therefore suitable for dianthus), composted grass clippings, pine needles and rotted manure are all suitable. Stable horse manure—if you can get it—works well in heavy soils because of its high straw content. If you live close to the ocean where it's easy to access seaweed, you will find it beneficial.

Sandy soil, like clay soil, lacks humus, though the results it produces are different. While dianthus like the perfect drainage offered by sandy soils, plant nutrients are quickly leached out and instead of holding moisture—with the attendant risk of drowning plants—this kind of soil dries out so quickly that the plants run the risk of dying from thirst. So, once again, incorporating humus-forming materials will bulk up the soil and improve its ability to retain moisture and nutrients.

Creating raised beds is an excellent way to improve drainage—and "raised" does not necessarily mean to a great height. Provide an edging just two bricks high, top up the bed behind it with soil that includes plenty of humus and the drainage will be instantly improved.

Fertilizing
The prolific flowering habit of some modern dianthus, and particularly the annual dianthus, will be aided and abetted by soil enriched with fertilizers before

cates soil of acidic composition, with the level of acidity increasing as the number decreases. A reading above 7 indicates that the soil is more alkaline, and the higher the number, the higher the alkalinity. In areas that tend to be acidic, for example, where a lot of leaf mold has been incorporated or pine needles have fallen—treating the soil with dolomite or moderate amounts of lime will "sweeten" it (lift its pH). Kits or meters to test pH are available at most garden centers and are especially useful for determining the composition of the soil in a new garden.

Heathers do not usually live in the same neighborhood as dianthus, but what an interesting couple they make.

planting time. Well-rotted manure, blood meal and mushroom compost all supply valuable nutrients. A balanced manufactured fertilizer with an NPK in equal ratios is also suitable (10-10-10, for example, where N = nitrogen, P = phosphate, K = potassium). Information on its use is printed on the packaging and usually gives details about the quantities needed for varying plant families.

When your dianthus are coming into bloom, a liquid feed high in potassium helps to maintain strong stems and buds and increase the number of flowers. It also enhances their color. Plants in the *Dianthus* family, however, do not require rich soil and too much nitrogen will encourage soft foliage growth at the expense of flowers. (In the past, carnation growers who wanted perfect blooms for the show bench treated their plants with soot diluted in water to increase the size of the flowers and deepen their color.)

Controlled-release fertilizers help to take the guesswork out of feeding plants. Different varieties are available and the time over which they release their chemicals also differs, ranging from two or three months to two years. These fertilizers are especially practical for container planting and are often already an ingredient in commercial soil mixes. Useful in the garden too, they can be added to the soil when a patch is being prepared for the planting of any members of the carnation family. In their second and third years, plants will appreciate a supplementary liquid feed when new growth is starting.

For gardeners who prefer an organic approach, liquid fertilizer (or manure tea) made by diluting manure in sufficient water to produce a thin, weak brown solution is effective and easy to use, though care must be taken to dilute sheep and fowl manure sufficiently as they can be too rich. Water-soluble powder fertilizers containing seaweed and other beneficial, natural fertilizers are also widely available now.

To avoid any risk of burning the roots, fertilizers should be added only when the soil or potting mix is already moist.

Care
Garden pinks are described as perennial, but have a relatively short life as productive garden plants. After two or three seasons they tend to lose their

'White Lady' looks superb with the viola 'Maggie Mott'.

plants and you may need to firm them back into the soil. Check regularly to ensure that they remain well anchored. During a long, dry summer, give your dianthus a generous watering from time to time—preferably in the morning to avoid a humid atmosphere after nightfall. A trickle system that delivers water around the bases of the plants and directly to the roots is most effective. Dianthus can, however, withstand extended dry periods and will revive quickly once it rains.

In *Beth Chatto's Gravel Garden* (Viking, 2000), the author talks about the selection of plants for her experimental garden in one of the driest parts of England where rainfall rarely exceeds 20 in (50 cm) per year. After the initial planting, all were expected to survive with no supplementary irrigation. Dianthus feature in several of the beds described. During the extremely dry summer of 1995, she reports, her resolve not to irrigate nearly wavered, but she held firm until rains came in August, and the plants survived.

Mulching helps to retain moisture in the soil, but these plants of dry rocky places like freely circulating air. They don't appreciate being cosseted with a blanket of moisture-holding material bulked up right around their throats. If you must mulch, use a layer of scoria or pumice around your dianthus.

The modern varieties of repeat-flowering pinks need to be pinched back when still young plants, to produce more flowering shoots. "Pinching" (also called "stopping") is a term used most often in relation to the commercially produced perpetual carnations. Simply stated, pinching means what its says—pinching out the growing tip of a plant's main stem to encourage side shoots. With most dianthus, the whole stem needs to be removed (not just the growing tip).

Repeat-blooming varieties also need deadheading—removing spent blooms—after each flush to promote further flowering. Remove the stems as well as the heads.

vigor and flower less prolifically. It's a good idea to take cuttings and replace your plants approximately every three years. New ones can be grown from seed, but remember that named varieties will not come true to type.

Pinks are hardy. Many will survive where winter temperatures sink as low as -40°F (-40°C) (to zone 3), though losses may occur when there is a sudden drop in temperature before an expected snowfall. On the other hand, they do not like excessive warmth and humidity. Where some dianthus will be quite happy in zone 10 in the temperate western U.S., they will have less chance of survival in zone 10 in the hotter southeast.

Frosts during severe winters can dislodge young

CHAPTER 6

Planting Ideas

Think carnations or pinks and inevitably you think flowers. Easy to grow, easy to propagate, they have long been valued as the ideal cottage-garden plant, with the focus, of course, on the flowers. But this is only one kind of garden where they fit easily.

In reality, dianthus suit a wide range of planting styles. They're tough, hardy plants that thrive on beach or dry, hillside gardens, and the smaller types are excellent in rock gardens or walls. Given their flexibility, it's time to think about dianthus as designer plants.

Stop a moment and consider their foliage. Narrow, sword-shaped, gray-green, gray-blue, sometimes even silver—and rarely disfigured by bugs—it can be stunning. In particular, the often dense, clumping habit of pinks makes them attractive, year-round plants. There's a place for them in today's gardens where the emphasis is on foliage. They have a role to play in providing texture.

It is not difficult to create an effect with flowers. Color in the garden, especially masses of color, draws comments, regardless of the design of the planting. By virtue of its impact, color is itself the design. If all else fails to satisfy in a garden plan, masses of color will rescue it.

If you are interested in creating a garden where the plants make satisfying patterns, even without flowers, it takes careful observation and planning. It's a matter of combinations. Think shape and form. Think complementary and contrasting: hard and soft, tall and short, round and spiky, feathery

Above: Nepeta and modern pinks—color that sings.

and stark. Snip samples of dianthus foliage and wander around your garden, testing their effect for color and shape against established plants. Visit a garden center where dianthus are sold in pots. Pick them up and group them experimentally beside other plants.

Imagine dianthus as ground cover—as a carpet, for example, in front of taller plants. This is the place to use them in bulk. Given the ease with which dianthus grow from cuttings, it need not be an expensive exercise. Santolinas, lavenders,

Dianthus 'Ian' makes a dramatic show in early summer.

astelias, honeywort (*Cerinthe major*) with its blue-tinged foliage and dark flowers, and *Helichrysum petiolare* all make good companion plants—though beware the smothering tendencies of helichrysum.

Dianthus can be useful plants for difficult situations. The old-fashioned pinks, in particular, thrive where soil is poor. Their slender, spiky foliage introduces a change of texture among other silver-gray plants with broad leaves, such as *Stachys byzantina* (syn *S. olympica*), or indented leaves like those of *Chrysanthemum maritima* and *Anthemis cupaniana*, plants that likewise do not fuss about dry, poor soil. (In fact, gray foliage plants tend to develop their best color—that is, their palest shades—in open, sunny situations with poor soils.) Add a bush or two of purple-leafed sage (*Salvia officinalis* 'Purpurascens') for contrast and immediately you have an interesting planting that will look good so long as the foliage lasts. In early summer, the rounded pink flowers of the dianthus combined with the mauve-blue of the spiky sage flowers lift this design to another level.

Opposite my front door I have a small patch of difficult garden. Camellia bushes take any goodness out of the soil, summer or winter it gets no sun and during summer it is usually very dry. One year I planted some big, glaucous echeverias, someone's surplus I had found at the landfill. The following year I added cuttings of an unnamed dianthus that had sprawled over a wall elsewhere in the garden. The dianthus has never flowered, but now the two plants, so different in shape but so similar in color, form a mat that draws a smile of satisfaction each time I walk out the front door. Just remember that echeverias need protection from too much hard rain or frost.

In the perennial border

A border planting implies a bed that is backed by a wall, fence or hedge and which fronts onto a lawn or other surface, perhaps a gravel area. It may be of irregular width—several yards (meters) wide in some places, narrower in others. Usually, lower plants form the front of the border and the plants rise in height progressively toward the back, though tall, bold, standout plants here and there can add an interesting, unexpected element. Pinks, however, do not fit this example. They are clump-forming and, as such, are most effective when planted in groups. Single dianthus, planted individually about a garden lack impact.

Two modern garden pinks harmonize effortlessly.

Before placing any variety of dianthus in the border, take stock of the plant's attributes. Consider the range of colors available. They come in white and every conceivable shade of pink; the colors that combine well with those plants we think of as cottage-garden plants. They also come in apricot, salmon and peach tones, which fit well with blues and purples, but often don't seem to fit with pink and red. Then there are the deep, dark crimson flowers that add a touch of excitement to any planting. Pale and subtle or garishly bright, dianthus can be planted in large gardens in masses of single or coordinated color waves. In small gardens, modest groups can provide a color accent or participate in an overall blend of shades.

Dianthus flowers are small to medium in size. On modern garden pinks, they're often carried in profu-

Above: Complementary colors and flower shapes make these pinks and verbenas eye-catching companions.

Above: For gardeners who like strong contrasts, try *Artemisia stelleriana* 'Mori's Choice' and *Dianthus barbatus* 'Sooty' ('Nigricans').

sion, so planting them closely where the blooms will mingle creates the greatest show of color, especially if you choose cultivars with a common flowering season.

Low-growing garden pinks are ideal at the front of the border. The old-fashioned types planted in an unplanned medley have the ability to harmonize into an interesting "tapestry," giving the effect of an Impressionist painting. Add scabious, a selection of flowering thymes, violas or the taller *Nigella* (love-in-the-mist), for example, and the color scheme is broadened.

Behind the above combination is the place for medium-height perennials, such as mauve-flowering catmint (*Nepeta*), wallflowers, hardy geraniums, and stoechas lavenders, which make fitting companion plants for probably all varieties of pinks. These lavenders usually have a neat habit and their range of purples and mauves complements the colors of dianthus. The taller pinks that form large clumps—'Ian', a free-flowering *Dianthus allwoodii* type is a good example—and border carnations fit among the perennials, where their long stems will get some support. 'Otaki Pink' is a carnation that originated in Australia as 'Frank Alldritt' and is one of my favorites. A heartstoppingly delicate pink, it has large, full-petaled, perfumed flowers—just like the carnations our grandmothers grew. 'Greytown', cerise and gray and a Keith Hammett hybrid, is more adventurous in its shading, although it echoes the colors of much earlier breeds of carnation.

For a vertical dimension among these bushy or clumping plants, perhaps add foxgloves, lilies or verbascum (mullein). The result of this kind of planting is summer-colorful, fragrant and attractive to bees.

As edgings

Don't forget to use pinks as edging plants. You might want to choose a perfumed cultivar if the edging frames a pathway where people frequently pass. Unlike scented foliage that needs to be

Border carnations that tend to flop and sprawl are best tucked in among other perennials that can lend support.

crushed to liberate its fragrance, perfumed flowers are much more generous with their favors.

But maybe the color of the blooms is more important to you than their perfume. There's no doubt a long, closely planted row of one cultivar in bloom can create a striking feature. Think though about its appearance once the flowers have faded. Where there is enough space, it's probably better to back an edging of your chosen cultivar (boasting attractive foliage, of course) with a contrasting plant to provide season-long interest. For an unusual but eye-catching display, visualize a low-growing row of neatly clumping dianthus with cerise flowers bordered by black mondo grass (*Ophiopogon planiscarpus* 'Nigrescens').

Along a pathway or drive is an excellent place to showcase laced cultivars, with their intricate markings, and small rock-garden types also make effective edging plants. I have seen 'Pink Jewel' (probably synonymous with 'Tiny Rubies'), tiny and tightly textured, follow the line of a paved driveway in a gentle curve. In early summer their minute, bright pink flowers make a brilliant display. For a short period, once the flowers are over, the plants look untidy, but after a quick deadheading, a neat, self-sufficient border remains for the rest of the year.

The top of a retaining wall is another appropriate place to use dianthus as edging plants. What better opportunity is there to use the larger, sprawling varieties? The wall provides a place where they can drape themselves with no need for support and, if it is at head height, they offer the beauty of their flowers and perfume at close range to anyone passing by.

Small pinks make ideal plants among rocks.

In the rock garden

The more compact forms of dianthus are very attractive merely for the neat mounds they create. Some close-textured alpine species resemble moss—rather spiky moss to be sure—but they make interesting companions for plants such as saxifrages or succulents that also grow in tight clumps and enjoy life in containers or troughs. Combined with a selection of low-growing, clumping dianthus, their circular forms provide contrast. These are plants for people who like playing with texture and subtly blending shades of green in their gardens.

Dianthus deltoides, plus its many cultivars, doesn't fit the description of a compact clump but it does make a neat, dark green mat and covers itself with bright flowers over many months. It can look enchanting among other rock-garden plants. It also self-seeds easily, squeezing up through cracks in paving where the crimson flowers of the species provide a luminous contrast against gray stone, especially at dusk when the light is fading.

Pinks with *Dianthus gratianopolitanus* (the Cheddar pink) in their parentage enjoy living in limestone areas. Planted at the top of rock walls, they soon spill over, their flowers making a fountain of pink in early summer and their foliage forming a textured fabric that softens the stone for the rest of the summer.

Container planting for decks and patios

Planting in containers is an exciting, fun way to show off plants and put interesting combinations together in a highly visible position. The increasing trend to sell plants at retail outlets only when they have reached the flowering stage encourages this use.

Compact forms of the garden pink *Dianthus plumarius*, recognizable by their narrow gray leaves, make very good container plants for use on decks and patios. This is especially true for repeat-flowering cultivars, such as 'Far Cry' (syn 'Baby Blanket'). Many of the plants that work well in rock gardens

Above: Dianthus foliage makes the perfect background for a colorful container planting of annual dianthus, ageratum, lobelia and perennial dianthus.
Left: Rock garden pinks grow happily with succulents.

also suit pot culture. Ensure that the potting mix is free-draining, but also take care that it is never allowed to completely dry out. Feeding with a liquid fertilizer from time to time will help keep the plants healthy.

The advantage of container planting is that plants can be moved around easily to reorganize color arrangements or landscaping effects. They can be brought into prominence when in flower and moved to obscurity if they start to look untidy. For creative gardeners, container plantings are a great incentive to experiment. Rather like flower arranging, it's easy to explore the possibilities of color combinations and the use of form and shape—and easy to change if the first attempt doesn't please.

An unusual pink—the Ise dianthus

The Ise (pronounced ee-say) dianthus is an example of a plant as an art form. Curiously, while breeders in the West strove to develop strains of *Dianthus* with rounded petals, gradually eliminating the fimbriated appearance of old pinks, the Japanese went the opposite way. Their breeding focused on producing a plant with ever longer, ever more finely "shredded" petals that shimmer down from the heart of the flower. The Ise dianthus was apparently developed from *D. chinensis* and a native Japanese species and dates from the middle of the 17th century, coinciding with the Edo period (1615–1868). The flower was developed over many generations by the Kishu clan who lived in the Kii district, encompassing present-day Wakayama, Ise, Tanabe and Shingu.

After the Meiji restoration in 1868, when the Emperor regained control over the warlords, this curious flower all but disappeared from view, its cultivation restricted to the Royal Court. Plants are easy to grow in pots, but do need overhead protection. A sheltered patio or a greenhouse is ideal. Not long-lived, Ise dianthus can be propagated by seed or from cuttings.

The Ise dianthus.

A type of carnation suited to growing outdoors in pots, but still not very common outside of Europe, is the "trailing carnation," often seen in window boxes, especially in Switzerland. Sometimes called the "Tyrolean trailing carnation," it needs to be grown in elevated containers, such as window boxes, hanging baskets or wall niches, to fully exploit its special characteristic. Plants of this type are best raised from cuttings, but occasionally seed is offered for sale.

Year-round good looks: dianthus foliage and echeverias.

Hypertufa troughs

Rock-garden pinks look superb growing in old stone troughs but not everyone is able to source one of these. However, it is fun and easy to make lookalikes in hypertufa.

Materials for a rectangular or square container
- 2 strong cardboard cartons—one 2 in (5 cm) smaller on all sides
- 2 or 3 drainage plugs, approx. 1 in (2 cm) in diameter and 2 in (5 cm) long, made from doweling, rolled cardboard or some similar material
- several heavy blocks or bricks
- 2 parts (by volume) peat
- 1 part (by volume) cement of any type
- 1 part (by volume) builder's sand. Pebbles or shells can be mixed in to add texture
- water to mix

Construction
- Place the larger carton on a firm, flat surface and surround it with blocks to support the sides.
- Dry mix the sand, peat and cement.
- Add water and mix to the consistency of stiff dough.
- Place a minimum 2-in (5-cm) layer of mix in the base of the carton.
- Set the drainage plugs firmly into the base layer.
- Place the smaller carton on top of the mix inside the bigger carton.
- Place blocks inside the smaller carton, for weight.
- Fill in the gaps between cartons with the cement mix. It needs to be tamped down several times to rid the mix of air bubbles, but take care not to cause the sides to bulge out of shape.

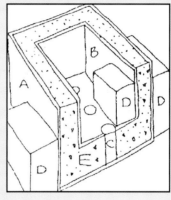

A tiny rock dianthus and summer-blooming 'Brook Cottage' are at home with succulents in a hypertufa pot.

A = outer carton
B = inner carton
C = drainage plug
D = heavy block
E = trough mix

- Leave in a dry, cool place for 2 or 3 nights until well hardened.
- In hot weather hose down the mold occasionally to prevent fast curing and possible cracking of the mix.
- When the mix is firm to the touch, gently remove the blocks, cardboard and plugs.
- Brush the outer sides with a wire brush to smooth the edges and simulate carved stone.
- Do not move or plant until completely cured, about 4 to 5 days

Planting
Use a gritty potting mix to fill the trough. Add controlled-release fertilizer if the ready-made potting mix you are using does not already contain such fertilizer, and plant with a selection of small dianthus, succulents, creeping thyme, and saxifrage.

CHAPTER 7

Carnations for Today's Florists

It seems ironic that the carnation best known around the world for its form, is the one least grown by home gardeners. Rarely grown outdoors, the perpetual-flowering carnation made its debut in France around the middle of the 19th century and, as its name implies, it never stops flowering—provided, of course, it receives favorable care.

These are the flowers you buy in the florist's shop, the blooms that last for up to three weeks in water and the flowers that became immortalized as buttonhole adornments in the days when British bankers brightened up their dark suits with a fresh flower.

Not only British bankers, however, sported carnations in their buttonholes. They were also the favorite flower of President McKinley. Legend has it that a close friend of his in Ohio grew repeat-flowering carnations as a commercial crop in the latter part of the 19th century and it was he who introduced them to McKinley. A scarlet carnation worn in his buttonhole became a talisman on the campaign trail leading to his election as President in 1896.

In 1901 McKinley attended the Pan-American Exposition in Buffalo wearing, as usual, his scarlet buttonhole. A little girl in the receiving line to meet the President confided to him that her schoolmates would have trouble believing that he had actually shaken her hand. "Take my carnation," he said, unpinning it from his lapel. "Show it to them and they'll know you were telling the truth." The

little girl walked away with the well-known talisman as the man next in line to greet the President pulled out a gun and shot him. Not long afterwards, the carnation became recognized as the state flower of Ohio.

As with many members of the *Dianthus* genus, the early genealogy of the perpetual-flowering carnation is clouded with varying versions. Some say its parent was the result of a cross between an unnamed Flemish carnation and the Mayonnais or de Mahon carnation, a remontant or repeat-flowering variety requiring no dormancy period, that was raised in France in the mid-1700s. Some believe it was derived

Opposite: Like many of today's perpetual carnations, these were bred in Holland.
Above right: Deep pink is always popular for carnations.

from a cross between the Indian pink *Dianthus chinensis* and *D. caryophyllus*. There are also suggestions that its branching characteristics and its great height are evidence of *D. arboreus* ancestry. (*D. arboreus*, the tree carnation, comes from Greece.)

During the second half of the 19th century, growers, mainly French but resident both in their home country and in New York, made crosses between various types of remontant carnations, producing named varieties that were sought after in the cut-flower markets of the time.

One cultivar which maintained its popularity for over a century was the blush-pink 'Souvenir de Malmaison', so called because of its similarity to the rose of the same name. It was a remontant carnation, raised in France in 1857, that gave birth to a range of perpetuals which first appeared as seedlings in the early years of the 20th century. Shorter than other perpetual carnations, they formed bushy plants bearing very large flowers with a strong fragrance and a color range limited to various shades of pink.

'A. Alégatière' was a scarlet self, named after its breeder and described as a tree carnation. It caused a sensation when it appeared in the 1860s. About the same time the first good, yellow-ground, perpetual-flowering carnation was bred by an American-based Frenchman named Donati. He called it 'Victor Emmanuel'.

Perhaps the biggest stir, however, was created by the rose-pink cultivar 'Mrs. Thos. W. Lawson' raised by Scotsman Peter Fisher in 1895, and five years later reputedly sold to the American copper baron Thomas W. Lawson for the enormous sum of $30,000. This carnation brought with it stronger stems, strong calyxes and a free-flowering habit that extended over the Scottish winter. It was the forerunner of the true perpetual-flowering varieties and became the parent of several other cultivars, all famous in their time.

Fisher started his working life as an apprentice gardener at the age of 15, emigrated to the United States, where he set up several nurseries in Massachusetts and grew and sold carnations there for more than 30 years. Another cultivar of his breeding, the blush pink 'Enchantress', was a star at Covent Garden Market in London in 1905.

These early, perpetual-flowering varieties established the U.S. in the forefront of commercial production for the cut-flower trade until the latter years of the 20th century. Now however, while there are still sizeable commercial growers in California and Colorado, the bulk of production has moved to South America, Israel, Kenya and back to several European countries.

It took another three decades before the next breakthrough occurred in the improvement of commercial varieties and it was another emigrant Scot, William Sim, who created the impetus. Unfortunately, he died before the enormous impact from his breeding program became apparent.

A modern carnation with traditional form.

The Sim Story

William Sim was born in Scotland in 1869 and at the age of 11 began work as an apprentice gardener. He learned about soils and greenhouse culture and how to grow fruit and vegetables. When he was 18 he emigrated to the United States where he set up a small greenhouse operation in Saugus, near Boston. He began growing snapdragons and violets, chrysanthemums, sweet peas and tomatoes, then added primroses, cucumbers and roses. By 1906 he had eight greenhouses with a total glass area of 75,000 square feet (23,000 square meters). World War I erupted and markets changed. To survive in business after the war, Sim too had to change. With a huge area of well-fed soil at his disposal, he looked around for a plant he thought would fit with the swinging twenties. Carnations were the answer.

Soon the Sim Carnation Company became well known for its cut flowers, its cuttings and some noteworthy cultivars that William bred. It wasn't long before he sold the flower-production business and moved to Maine, where he concentrated on breeding. Through the thirties he showed his flowers every year at the American Carnation Society conventions. In 1938 he produced a promising bright red seedling. At his son's suggestion he named it 'Farida' after the young queen of Egypt.

When William Sim died unexpectedly in 1940 he left many untested seedlings in his greenhouses. His business was taken over by Harold Potter from Massachusetts, who renamed the brilliant red seedling 'William Sim' in memory of its creator. Outstanding features of the plant include its vigorous growth, its long, strong stems, large blooms and free-flowering habit. Only becoming evident later was its amazing ability to throw sports—possibly as many as 200—in almost every color except crimson.

The progeny of 'William Sim' were widely developed for the next 30 years. Some grow to almost 5 ft (1.5 m) tall and Sim cultivars are featured consistently in catalogs throughout the carnation-growing world. Unfortunately, the calyxes of Sims are prone

Above: A superb white carnation.

Above: A perpetual carnation for those who love pastels.

to splitting, but, more seriously, the plants are not resistant to fusarium wilt and in their turn they have been largely superseded by more modern varieties, bred for their disease resistance.

Spray carnations: widely used by florists and long-lasting as cut flowers.

After the Sims

Spray carnations originated in the United States in the early 1950s and, like many momentous discoveries, were purely the result of chance. W. Pomeroy Thomson, a grower in Connecticut, had for many years collected samples of new perpetual and standard carnation cultivars grown by his friends. He trialed them in a small greenhouse reserved for this purpose. Returning once from a long trip, he found the trial house totally neglected. Among the plants, none of which had been disbudded, was a small standard called 'Exquisite'. Its color combination of palest pink and a striking violet-purple was eye-catching, but more striking than the color was the elegant spray of flowers it exhibited. Pomeroy Thomson took a vase of the flowers to a florist where they immediately aroused considerable interest.

It wasn't long before Thomson was growing 'Exquisite' on a larger scale for commercial production. Later he developed several interesting sports of 'Exquisite' and the first family of spray carnations—sometimes called miniature carnations—was born.

Thomson was quick to see the possibilities of these new-generation plants. His subsequent breeding program produced a number of families of sprays and though their initial introduction into the American market met with some resistance, they are now widely grown on both sides of the Atlantic, often outdoors. They come in many attractive color combinations and have largely replaced the Sims. Like their forbears, they are grown for the cut-flower market. Few amateurs grow them.

Spray carnations are a smaller version of the standard perpetual-flowering variety and if fed correctly can produce up to ten blooms per stem. They need to be pinched back once, and disbudding is only necessary to remove the crown bud. Blooms are therefore smaller than those of standard perpetuals, ranging in size from 1 to 2 in (2.5 to 5 cm) across, but they are much more numerous and this is their appeal. One stem can fill a vase.

Characteristics of perpetual-flowering carnations

Also known as standard carnations, these plants will flower year-round, given suitable conditions. Their life span is about two years and commercial growers tend to continually replace their stock on a rotating basis. Less hardy than border carnations, they like airy conditions and a dry atmosphere. Excessive humidity is their enemy. When temperatures are too high, the flower size reduces; when it is too cold, the flowers don't always open completely. Cold and rain damage blooms, and frost kills these carnations, so it's easy to see why they are best grown under cover.

Stems are much longer than are those of border carnations. They are strong and wiry, sometimes growing to 28 in (70 cm) and they need staking. Flowers may be as large as 3 in (8 cm) across, with smooth, fringed and picotee petals.

Modern breeding of carnations for commercial purposes aims at producing plants that are disease resistant, with particular attention to fusarium wilt, and this is the great advantage spray carnations have over the older varieties of perpetual-flowering types. Also important are a longer productive season, a uniform yield and a wider range of colors, shapes and forms. In Europe, Israel and South America breeding of commercial carnations continues apace and the Mediterranean types are at present the most developed.

Carnations in the greenhouse

Home gardeners with a greenhouse are able to provide the conditions that perpetual-flowering and spray carnations enjoy. They are plants that like growing in pots and, provided the temperature is maintained at a warm enough level, the thrill of

Above: An arresting "party dress" color combination.

Above: Perpetual carnations come in a wide range of clear-colored selfs, such as this warmly toned example.

being able to bring a container of blooming plants indoors in winter tempts some gardeners to grow these varieties under cover. If grown in greenhouse beds, rather than in pots, they are more prone to disease.

Planting

It is easiest to start with rooted cuttings of named varieties. Plant them individually into 3-in (8-cm) well-drained pots. As carnations do not like wet feet, and soggy soil can lead to stem rot, care must be taken to provide a mix that is always free-draining. Commercial potting mixes are readily available, but choose a formula that it is open, porous and gritty. For those who like to mix their own, the following recipe is uncomplicated: 2 parts sterilized soil, 3 parts sharp sand, 3 parts peat, controlled-release fertilizer.

Start the potted cuttings in diffused sunlight— they can be protected with newspaper or shadecloth for the first two or three days—after which it is safe to allow them full exposure to the sun. The ideal night temperature range is 58–60° F (14–16° C) and on sunny days good ventilation is necessary to prevent excessive heat in the greenhouse, except when there is severe frost, of course. During hot summer weather protect the plants against excessive heat. In zone 7 and warmer, greenhouses will need to be shaded to prevent the foliage scorching. Good light is important in all seasons and to keep perpetuals in flower over winter the temperature should not go below 50° F (10°C).

Pinching and disbudding

When the plant has eight or nine pairs of leaves, it is time for the first pinching. This encourages the growth of side shoots and therefore more flowering stems. Snap off the growing tip, leaving five or six pairs of leaves. Approximately two weeks later, new side shoots should have appeared, sprouting from the leaf axils.

About this time, too, the roots should have penetrated the mix to the outsides of the pot and will perhaps show signs of emerging through the bottom holes. This means the young plants are ready to move into larger pots. Transfer them into 6–7 in (15–18 cm) pots and insert a stake alongside each plant for support when it is flowering.

Modern perpetual carnations.

Many growers pinch their plants a second time when the new shoots are long enough to have the top two or three sets of leaves nipped out, once again leaving five or six pairs. Flowers usually appear between five and six months after pinching, so the timing of this operation will determine the flowering sequence of the plants, an important consideration for commercial growers. Shoots that are left unpinched flower earlier, but less abundantly.

Disbudding is a technique used to increase the size of flowers. Perpetual-flowering carnations are admired for their large blooms; so they are usually disbudded. This reduces the number of flowers per stem but ensures that the one bloom remaining will be as big as possible. To disbud, simply remove the

thin side stalks every few days as they develop, leaving only the crown bud to develop on each flowering stem.

If it is spray carnations that you are growing, however, then the reverse is true. Nip out the crown bud only, leaving other stalks intact, to encourage multiple blooms on the stem.

Watering

Plants potted in soil are less likely to drain as evenly as those grown in soil-less compounds, such as mixtures of peat, sand, and perlite, for example. In summer it is important to prevent the plants from drying out completely. The surface of the mix is an indication: if it is dry, insert your finger a few inches (several centimeters) into the compost to test the moisture below the surface. If it feels damp, water-

ing can wait. If it is dry, water your plant. Small plants can be gently knocked out of the pot to check for moisture around the root area, but take care not to damage the roots.

Once you decide to water, it is important that it seeps right through the mix and does not merely wet the visible surface. Once again, the finger test is fairly reliable. Remember, too, that clay pots dry out faster than plastic.

Water early in the day to allow foliage to dry off and avoid scorching by sun, and to avoid unnecessary humidity at night. As summer wanes and the weather becomes cooler, plants require less watering and by mid-winter, established plants prefer to be kept relatively dry.

Feeding

Provided the original potting mix was enriched with fertilizer, potted plants will not need further feeding until the buds start to appear. From then until late autumn, feeding "little and often" works well. Dilute a balanced fertilizer in water, according to the instructions on the package, and use this mixture at watering time. If the soil has dried out, however, wet it thoroughly before adding any fertilizer, for it may burn the roots when applied directly to dry plants.

Give plants growing in an unheated greenhouse in winter one high-potash feed in mid-fall, or you can sprinkle a controlled-release fertilizer around the root area. Plants overwintering in warmth should also receive a monthly, high-potassium feed.

When spring comes, any strongly growing plants will need to be repotted into bigger containers, 8 or 9 in (20 or 23 cm). Start feeding again at biweekly intervals, once they have had a few weeks to settle into their new pots. By early summer this can be increased to weekly feeding. Heating in many areas can be discontinued in late spring when daylight has increased and night temperatures have risen to above 50°F (10°C).

CHAPTER 8

Carnations Indoors

In pots

In large cities many plants sold in pots, in flower, are effectively a bunch of flowers with roots. Many such items are bred specifically with the expectation that the consumer will discard them when the flowers are past their best. They are not expected to perform in the garden. Those longing for summer use them to briefly stave off winter; dinner guests buy them as presents for the host; friends and family take them to cheer up a hospital patient.

Some garden pinks are marketed for this purpose, and there are also some strains of pink based on the annual or short-lived *Dianthus sinensis*, like the Kopo Series developed in the Netherlands, that have been bred in greenhouses with short production time and are meant for a brief, but attractive, life in a pot. They look superficially similar to compact forms of *D. plumarius*, but they can be recognized as being of *D. chinensis* origin by their broader leaves, which tend to be green rather than gray. Also in this category is a breed of dwarf carnations raised from cuttings.

In the same way that plants mutate (or sport) for flower color, mutations can occur that affect other parts of the plant. One such mutation allows the development of dwarf plants. This is the origin of the Adorable and Romance Series developed by the California Florida Plant Company. A mutation was first noted around 1982 in some spray-carnation seedlings being developed by general manager Oscar Hasegawa and plant breeder Walter Jessel. Originally, Hasegawa intended to throw out the dwarf mutant, but a woman customer saw it and said, "How adorable!" It was saved and ultimately developed, by means of a long-term breeding program, into the Adorable Series.

A more recent development has been the Romance Series. This resulted from back-crossing to spray carnations to produce slightly taller plants with more blooms. Both strains are excellent and are the ultimate "bunch of flowers with roots." Like

Bred for indoor decor, potted miniature carnations are popular new plants.

the potted chrysanthemums with which we are all familiar their primary purpose is as houseplants.

Various seed strains such as the Japanese Lillypot Series are superficially similar to the Adorable Series, but they have been developed from annual type seed strains. They are mainly sold as "instant color" items in retail outlets, are short-lived and soon make an untidy plant in the garden.

In vases
One of the joys of growing carnations and pinks is the supply of cut flowers they provide. Carnations, in particular, have a long vase life. In fact, commercially grown carnations will last up to three weeks so long as the water is kept fresh. It helps to recut the stems each time the water is changed.

When picking carnations or pinks for the house, early morning is the best time. Choose blooms that

Perpetual carnations: florists' flowers for the 21st century

are not fully open. Breaking the stem is probably better for the plant than cutting it as a stub left behind may become an entry point for fungus. Stems break easily at a node. As soon as possible after picking, plunge the flowers up to their necks in a container of cool water and leave them for several hours.

Lemonade, ASA, sugar or citric acid (e.g., 1 tsp/5 mL of lemon juice per 2 pints/1 L of water) are all reputed to help prolong vase life and, of course, blooms will last longer in a cool room, away from direct sunlight. Make sure the length of stem immersed in water is stripped of leaves. Vases of flowers placed next to a bowl where apples are stored will tend to wilt quickly because of the ethylene emitted by the ripening fruit.

CHAPTER 9

Propagation

A satisfying aspect of growing dianthus is the ease with which they can be propagated. Garden pinks look great when several varieties are grown in adjacent clumps that spread and mingle to form a raised carpet of color. And this look is easy to achieve in a short time—in fact, the plants can do it all themselves, for they set seed freely.

In a few seasons your dianthus will have self-seeded readily, with an interesting blending of color as varieties hybridize among themselves. However, if you're a gardener who likes to plot and plan, you'll probably want to take a hand in the color scheme and raise plants to fit your own landscape design.

Border carnations are propagated by taking cuttings or by layering; pinks by sowing seed or from cuttings; annual carnations and sweet Williams are acquired most easily from seed. If you want clones of cultivars, then vegetative propagation, i.e., layering or taking cuttings, are the only ways to ensure that offspring will match parents. Species will come true from seed.

Seeds and sowing

The best germination rates are achieved when the seed of border carnations, annuals and pinks is fresh. The seed is held in an upright capsule formed inside the dried calyx. When ripe, it's easy to shake out. Seeds need no special treatment before sowing, though their coating is brittle and they should be handled carefully. If you are gathering your own seeds and want to store them for later use, ensure that they are kept dry and cool in a dark place.

Pinks can be sown directly into open ground in late spring, though you will get better results from

Above: The field carnation 'Frank Aldritt' was hybridized in the 1930s.
Opposite: 'Sunny'

early indoor sowing. Cultivate the soil so that its texture is finely crumbled and consistent. Sow the seeds thinly, barely cover with a light layer of fine soil and keep it moist until the first sign of green appears above ground. When the seedlings are large enough to handle, thin them and protect from disturbance by birds, cats or enthusiastic weed sleuths in your family.

Sweet Williams grow easily from seed.

Seed is best sown in trays of seed-raising mixture and lightly covered by fine vermiculite or a fine layer of sand. Mist with water and place the tray in a warm position. The soil mix must remain moist to ensure germination, which can be rapid, with the first seedlings appearing within 4–5 days. They should be grown in good light from the outset to ensure compact, sturdy seedlings. If grown in shade, they stretch and are much more prone to damage and damping-off (the failure of the seedling caused by fungi). Well-spaced seedlings, which allow for good air circulation, are also less likely to succumb to damping-off.

The first leaves to appear are cotyledons—i.e., seed leaves—that bear no resemblance to the mature grasslike leaves. When the true leaves appear, the seedlings are ready for pricking out or transferring to more spacious living quarters, usually a deeper tray.

The seedlings are very delicate at this stage—think of them as premature babies—and they need careful handling. Loosen the soil before attempting to dislodge them and hold them between thumb and forefinger by the seed leaves. Firm them into the soil to avoid air pockets and continue to keep the planting mix moist. When the plants are about 2 in (5 cm) high, they are ready to be transferred to small pots.

Gardeners with limited time, or those raising large numbers of seedlings, may find it easier to bypass the pricking-out process and plant the babies directly into small pots.

The young plants are ready for transplanting into permanent positions when the root structure has grown out to the limit of the mix in the pot, probably when they are about 6 in (15 cm) high. If you live in an area with a mild climate, it is best to plant out in the fall, but if you live in an area with a harsh winter, wait until the spring. If raised in a greenhouse, seedlings should be hardened off (acclimatized) by placing their pots in a sheltered, outside position for a few weeks prior to planting.

For gardeners who want numerous plants, it makes more sense to start them indoors and transplant them into the garden later as small, established plants to fit in with a landscaping plan. Indoor sowing means you are less dependent on favorable weather when the tiny seedlings are vulnerable to wind and cold. They can be sown under warm cover (60–70°F/15–20°C) in winter. Many pinks, planted from seeds, will flower in the same season.

Annual dianthus 'Strawberry Parfait'.

William Cobbett, that didactic gardener from the 19th century, gives precise advice about propagating sweet Williams:

The seed should be sown in an open bed in the spring and in rows, which should be kept hoed and weeded through the summer. In autumn plant them out where they are to blow [bloom], and do not put the plants nearer than within six inches of one another, either in beds or in clumps. If you wish to propagate a particular plant, you must do it by striking a cutting from one of the flower stalks; but this should be before that stalk has flowered. Let there be two joints to the cutting; and strike it under a handglass upon a little heat.

However, it is possible to have flowering sweet Williams in the same year of planting by sowing seeds indoors, as for pinks. By late spring they can be gradually hardened off and planted outdoors, where they will flower in summer.

Seeds of annual carnations will germinate in temperatures as low as 40°F (4°C), though it hap-pens more quickly in warmer conditions—two to three weeks at 65°–75°F (18–23°C)—and they will flower approximately 28 weeks from planting. Sow seed in late winter—the earlier you start them off, the earlier they will flower. The seedlings should be potted into shallow trays and planted outdoors in an open sunny situation once all danger of frost has passed. All their side shoots turn into flowering shoots in the season of planting and often they will continue blooming until the first frosts of fall, though it is essential to deadhead them from time to time.

Recipe for sterilizing seed-raising mix
Fill a baking dish with moist soil, seal the dish in an oven bag and "cook" at 185°F (85°C) for at least 30 minutes. Remove from the oven and cool before using.

Vegetative propagation
Layering

Border carnations were traditionally propagated by layering, garden pinks more rarely. Layering involves partially cutting the stem of a shoot and fastening it into the ground while it is still attached to the parent plant. This encourages roots to form at the cut node (or joint) in the stem.

The best time for layering is midsummer, or as soon as the plants have finished flowering and before the stems become brittle in autumn. Choose a healthy parent plant and select a robust, long shoot as the potential layer. Remove its lower leaves, leaving at least five pairs of leaves on the top part of the shoot. You will notice that the nodes on the upper part of the stem are closer together than near the base of the shoot. It is one of these upper nodes that should be split. Loosen the soil around the base of the mother plant and create a small pocket of planting mix that contains light soil and sharp sand. This is where the layer will be inserted in the ground.

Use a clean, sharp, pointed knife—one with a thin blade will make the job easier. Prepare the shoot to be layered by slicing the stem lengthwise through a node and forming a tongue. The stem should be slit for approximately $^1\!/_2$ in (1 cm) two nodes below where the leaves were stripped off. Fasten the tongued section into the ground with a wooden peg or a hooked piece of wire that will not cut into the stem. Firm the soil around the pegged layer and water well, making sure it never completely dries out while the roots are forming.

Layers take from four to six weeks to form roots, at which stage they can be severed from the mother plant. Once the umbilical cord is cut, leave the rooted layers in place for several days to stabilize before removing them. The newly planted layers will need protection from full sun until they are well established.

Some growers may prefer to bury a small pot, filled with planting mix, beside the mother plant

Shoot of a border carnation or tall garden pink, stripped and ready for layering.

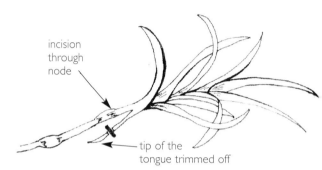

incision through node

tip of the tongue trimmed off

Shoot showing incision in the stem and the trimmed "tongue," prepared for pegging down.

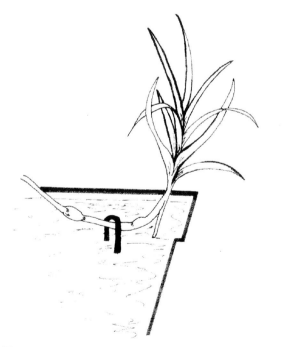

The prepared shoot layered into soil and pegged down.

and fasten the layer directly into it. This avoids the potting step once the layer has rooted and reduces disturbance to the layer. Make sure that the soil in the small pot does not dry out.

Above: 'Dawlish Joy', with its attractive, long, broad-leafed foliage is a carnation to propagate by layering.

Several layers can be taken from one mother plant, provided it is large enough.

Cuttings

All dianthus can be propagated by cuttings, though border, spray and perpetual-flowering carnations root more successfully when bottom heat is provided.

As with layering, the best time of the year to take cuttings of carnations and garden pinks is late summer when there is sufficient warmth and enough time for the cuttings to establish before cold weather arrives to inhibit their growth.

Cuttings for border carnations and pinks are best taken from non-flowering side shoots and should be short and sturdy—no more than 4 in (10 cm) long—and the healthier the mother plant, the better the quality of the cuttings will be.

It's tempting to take cuttings on the spur of the moment—to relieve the monotony of a weeding spree or when wandering in the garden admiring a

Above: 'Kesteven Kirkstead' dates from the 1970s.

Rock garden pinks such as 'Mary' are easily propagated from cuttings.

plant with a friend, but plan ahead and your success rate will be greater. Water the mother plant the previous day and cuttings will be more succulent, more inclined to form roots easily. If you take the trouble to fetch a sharp knife or secateurs, there will be less risk of damage to the parent plant.

Where only a few new plants are required, the cuttings may be planted directly into the garden, but it is easier to take care of developing plants when they're set out near your working area in trays or pots. Strip off the lower two pairs of leaves from each cutting before inserting them in the planting mix. The following media are all suitable: clean sand, a mixture of equal parts soil (or compost) and sand, or equal parts perlite, sand and peat. (Never use sand from an ocean beach as the salt content is too high.) The cuttings need to be inserted about 2 in (5 cm) apart.

Place the cuttings in a shaded area, keep the planting mix moist and roots should develop in four to six weeks. Roots will form more quickly in warm humid weather.

Damping-off can be a problem, not only with seedlings but also with cuttings. Sterilized soil helps to prevent this disease. Once cuttings have rooted, those set out in pure sand will need some nutrients. Either repot them in potting mix or compost or plant them out in permanent positions in the garden.

When the ground has been prepared outdoors, that is dug over, weeded and fertilized, dig a small hole and if your soil is poor or very gravelly, prepare a "nest" of compost and soil to encourage the new plant to develop strong roots. This is a good time to incorporate some slow-release fertilizer if you are using a homemade potting mix. Fill the hole with water. When this has drained away, it's time to plant. The cutting should be planted at the same level as it was in its pot and the soil needs to be firmed around it to eliminate air pockets.

In areas where frosts are persistent, the young plants will be happier in pots where they will receive some protection, such as in a cold greenhouse, on a veranda or under eaves.

Root divisions

Another vegetative method of propagating pinks is from rooted sections. This is most useful when you have made the decision that some old, ragged, but still cherished plants are really past their prime and have to go. You love the flowers, you've left it too late to take good cuttings and you're afraid you will lose them. Pull the plants apart as you take them out and trim the foliage. Tidy-up portions where there are healthy roots still attached and replant them.

CHAPTER 10

Pests, Diseases and Disorders

Healthy plants, like healthy people, are much less likely to succumb to disease than those that are stressed or raised in unfavorable conditions. Heredity, of course, is also important. Modern cut-flower carnation types are increasingly bred for disease resistance, so choice of variety has a part to play in the ultimate health of the plant. As discussed in Chapter 5 on cultivation, all members of the carnation family need a well-ventilated situation with free circulation of air, sharp drainage and plenty of sun. They don't like wet feet or damp, humid conditions. Cater to these needs and they will be well prepared to combat attack.

Dianthus and border carnations are generally easy-care plants and control of pests and disease poses few problems for home gardeners. The ease with which old garden pinks escape and multiply in the wild is proof of their tough constitution. Carnations grown in greenhouse conditions need more attention and should be checked regularly for evidence of pests, particularly on the undersides of leaves and in the tiny crevices around developing buds.

If you decide intervention is necessary, chemical insecticides act in two different ways. **Systemic pesticides**, usually applied by spraying leaves and stems, are absorbed by the plant and carried by the sap to all its living parts. Any insects sucking the sap will be killed. Systemic insecticides protect the plant for a specified length of time.

Contact insecticides are exactly that. They kill any insect they hit and are applied as sprays, dusts or smokes. Many of these contain Malathion, which is dangerous to humans. Less potentially damaging

Massed in a border, modern pinks make a wonderful display.

organic insecticides, containing pyrethrum, are available. Organic methods should also be considered.

Care must be taken at all times when dealing with chemical pesticides or fungicides. Used carelessly, they can be dangerous to humans and ani-

'Meridian'

mals; residues can remain in the soil for a long time, with the risk of entering into the food chain. It is important to follow the manufacturer's instructions, to always label containers used to dispense or handle pesticides and to keep them out of reach of children, preferably locked away when not in use. Protective clothing should be worn and care taken not to inhale any fumes. Merely washing a container after use does not necessarily remove all residues. What you remember using as a dispenser for insecticide may in fact have been used to hold weed killer. Next time you use the container, you don't want to kill the whole plant instead of only the insects on it!

Sprays are easily carried by wind, so choose calm weather and do any necessary spraying in the evening when bees are less active.

Remember that insecticides can't think: they are unable to distinguish between good bugs, such as ladybugs, and bad bugs, such as greenfly, which ladybugs eat. "How damaging are those insects?" we need to ask ourselves, before we reach for the killer sprays.

Just as bacteria that attack humans have developed resistance to antibiotics, there is a similar risk of bugs developing resistance to chemical killers.

Alternating between the types of chemicals you use—or between organic methods—will help to prevent this.

> **Organic anti-aphid spray**
> 1 lb (500 g) rhubarb leaves
> 3 pints (1.5 L) of water
> Simmer the leaves in the water for 30 minutes. Strain the mixture and store in a glass jar (this is now the rhubarb extract).
>
> When ready to use, add 1 fl oz (100 ml) of dishwashing liquid in 3 pints (1.5 L) of water and mix with the rhubarb extract.

Ants

The nectar of dianthus attracts ants and when the plants start to bloom, they climb into the open flowers for a feast.

If the petals of your carnations fall out and the flower collapses, blame ants—they could be nibbling on the center tips of the petals. Dusts containing pyrethrum or pirimiphos methyl will control them effectively.

Aphids (including greenfly)

All gardeners are familiar with greenfly, those tiny insects that swarm onto plants at the height of the growing season and greedily suck the sap, particularly from juicy young shoots, leaving sticky honeydew in their wake.

They multiply at an alarming rate and like other aphids they look unsightly, their sap-sucking habits debilitate plants and, most seriously, they often transmit virus from diseased plants to healthy ones. Virus disease becomes apparent in the form of yellow streaks or spots on the foliage.

If you grow only a few plants (and have amazing persistence) it may be possible to control these

'Pink Jewel', a tiny clumping dianthus with flowers on stems about 2 in (5 cm) tall.

annoying insects by physically squashing them on a continuing basis. Systemic pesticides are effective, but spraying will need to be repeated at regular intervals over summer. Some gardeners report success controlling aphids with an organic "tea" made from rhubarb leaves (see box).

Garlic planted beside dianthus outdoors in British Columbia has been found to deter some pests, including carnation fly (Galbally, 1997).

Birds, rabbits and mice

Birds will chew on carnations, especially in spring. The plants can be protected by stringing black thread above them. In rabbit-prone areas, wire-netting fencing, set well into the earth, is the best protection. Mice can sometimes be a problem in winter, eating plants in greenhouses. Use mouse-traps or the resident cat, so long as it is trained to treat flowerpots with due respect.

Carnation fly, leafminer or carnation maggot

This fly can be a problem on carnations and pinks grown outdoors. It lays its eggs on the foliage of the carnation. Once hatched, the maggots feed on tissues between the upper and lower skins of the leaves and create whitish tunnels in their progress towards the main growth, and eventually the central stem of the plant—hence the name "leafminer." If the tracks are visible on leaves, cut the leaves off and preferably burn them. Otherwise, try to extract the maggot before it can pupate in midsummer, ready to start the next life cycle.

Handpicking is effective where leaves or plants are already mined. Maldison or pirimiphos methyl-based sprays can help where damage is not too advanced. Planting garlic alongside plants may be an effective deterrent.

Caterpillars, including tortrix moth caterpillar

There is a range of caterpillars with varying habits. Some feed by day, others by night—when they can be sought by flashlight, picked off and squashed. Some are harder to find, secreting themselves inside the calyxes of carnations and pinks while they feed on flowers, born or unborn.

The tortrix moth caterpillar is cunning. It's almost as if nature knew it needed protection against modern spray chemicals, for the tortrix moth caterpillar has the ability to spin a fine web and roll the growing tips of the plant around itself as a shield, meanwhile growing plump and long ($3/4$ in/2 cm) on carnation foliage. The moth is tiny

and bright orange in color, an unexpected metamorphosis from the rather large caterpillar.

For control, use one of the following insecticides: maldison, acephate, carbaryl, pirimiphos methyl, permethrin or bifenthrin.

Cuckoo spit or spittlebug (sometimes called froghopper)

Another of the sapsucking variety, this insect is most visible by the frothy deposit it exudes as a sun-umbrella to shield the bug while it carries on its nefarious business. Usually seen in the junction between stem and leaf, this bug should be treated as for aphids if it becomes a real problem.

Earthworms

Not usually regarded as any kind of pest, earthworms nevertheless are a problem in pot culture where they have a restricted run. Their prolific casts tend to clog the soil and impede drainage. To remove them, first allow the soil to dry out, then irrigate the pot with water to which lime has been added. This causes the worms to come to the surface, where they can be picked off.

Earwigs

Nasty creepy-crawlies these—they chew buds and petals—but you can deal with them effectively and in an environmentally friendly way. Loosely fill pots with moss, straw, grass or even crumpled newspaper and set them out on their sides among the carnation plants for the earwigs to shelter in at night. Dispose of the critters on a daily basis.

Red spider mite

Just the mention of the red spider mite strikes dread into the heart of serious carnation growers. It is probably the most threatening enemy of the genus and is especially damaging in greenhouses, where it spreads quickly if unchecked. Yellow or brownish, rather than red, this spider is so small it can be seen only with the naked eye once it has formed

colonies, when it looks like a type of rust on the undersides of leaves. It attacks the leaves, puncturing the surface to suck out the contents.

The first indication of the mite's presence is usually the appearance of pale blotches on the upper leaf surface. The leaves lose their waxy covering, become dull, turn yellow and die. Once a plant is depleted of moisture, these ingenious invaders quickly move on. Unable to fly, they crawl to the top of the dying plant and start spinning furiously, creating an insect version of a mass bungy-jumping operation. This is not idle sport. The aerial "ropes" swing them across to the next healthy plant and they continue on their destructive passage.

Red spider mites thrive in hot, dry conditions. Shading the greenhouse to reduce temperatures and raising the level of humidity are two ways of creating conditions less conducive to the mites' prolific life cycle. Maximum ventilation is necessary, as humidity can encourage the growth of fungal infections. Simultaneously, treat the plants with acari-

Always popular, lavender complements the white blooms of 'Alan Titchmarsh'.

cides, spraying the foliage and watering the soil in the pot. Repeat the spraying every six or seven days to destroy the next cycle of mites.

The following ingredients are all effective acaricides: bifenthrin, propargite, dienochlor, abamectin, dicofol.

For those who prefer organic controls, there is the remedy suggested by Montagu Allwood in his *Carnations and All Dianthus* (1947):

…dissolve 1 ounce (25 g) of common salt in one gallon (4 liters) of water. This should be sprayed on in the early morning with a very fine spray, reaching every part of the plant, particularly the underside of the leaves, and a few hours after it should be washed off with the hose or syringe. This is not done with the idea of washing off the salt, for that would do no damage if it remained, but to wash off the red spider.

Slugs and snails

Dianthus foliage and stems are not particularly attractive to these slimy pests but where they are a problem, tempt them to their deaths with a saucer of stale beer. Alternatively, set out snail bait, protecting birds and pets by placing the bait in short pieces of broken drainpipe, small jars on their sides, or similar coverings.

Thrips

Like aphids, these tiny winged insects are sapsuckers. There are several varieties, but it is the onion thrip that attacks the unopened buds of carnations, leaving the flower to emerge with ugly, pale blotches where the color pigment has been sucked out.

Thrips breed outdoors in summer and in greenhouses during winter, laying their eggs on the calyx; the developing nymphs cause the damage. Thrips are especially prevalent during a hot dry period in summer. Either derris powder (if available), carefully applied to reach into folds in leaf and bud, or a systemic insecticide, will control this pest.

Wireworms

These pests are a threat to all plants and are especially prevalent in areas of grassland. About 1 in (2.5 cm) long and orange-yellow in color, they live in the soil for three to five years where they pupate, eventually appearing as a beetle. They munch plant roots—even burrowing up into the stems of carnations and dianthus—and cause death. An old-fashioned remedy is to bury pieces of potato or carrot just below the soil surface and mark them with sticks. The vegetables become infested with the worms and are easily removed and destroyed.

Diseases

Harmful fungi, bacteria and viruses cause disease. Home gardeners who grow their dianthus outdoors are unlikely to be seriously troubled by disease. Plants grown in greenhouses are more vulnerable and the results of continuing research on carnation diseases are of much more importance to commercial growers of perpetual-flowering carnations. In the early years of last century the dread disease of rust forced some carnation growers out of production. With increased knowledge and improved growing conditions, this is rarely a problem now.

The best defense in the greenhouse is always good hygiene combined with correct cultural conditions. Always check new plants before you buy them. Introducing diseased plants to healthy stock is a surefire method of spreading disease. The whole greenhouse should be disinfected once a year—preferably in the fall. Use an antibacterial and antifungal disinfectant at the recommended strength and wash down the glass walls, all the shelves and pots, and don't forget to also disinfect the tools you use.

Damping-off problems

This is one problem amateur gardeners need to be aware of—and it affects not only dianthus. Caused by a complex of fungi that spreads on the surface of the soil, damping-off attacks seedlings shortly after they emerge and form their first pair of leaves. Just when you are congratulating yourself on a good germination rate and admiring a prolific crop of tiny green plants, the fungi can hit. The stem is damaged at soil level, causing the seedling to collapse and rot. In the space of 24 hours a whole tray of seedlings can be destroyed. Overcrowding encourages damping-off, as does a high level of humidity. Use a fresh batch of sterilized seed-raising mix for each planting and avoid overwatering. Spraying the seed mix with a solution of copper oxychloride or a fungicide containing benomyl before and after sowing is helpful. New cuttings may also be affected by damping-off.

Altenaria

Caused by a fungus, this disease shows itself as pale brown lesions on the calyx that progress to the lower parts of the petals, eventually leading to col-

Dianthus deltoides 'Rosea'

lapse of the flower. Treat it with a fungicide containing benomyl.

Rust

This used to be perhaps the most common disease to attack dianthus. Should you notice the telltale signs—small, brownish marks on both sides of leaves that split open—it's time to act. Pick off the infected leaves, burn them and wash your hands before touching healthy plants. As with mildew, adequate ventilation will help prevent rust; it likes warm, damp conditions. Treat by spraying with copperoxychloride or dusting with a fungicide containing mancozeb.

Leaf spot

There are two forms of this disease: one is marked by small, purple spots with yellow margins that develop black powdery spores, eventually destroying whole leaves; the second causes brown spots with purple margins to develop on leaves and stems. Once again, warm, damp conditions are the enemy. Spray with copperoxychloride or a fungicide containing mancozeb.

Botrytis

Another disease caused by warm, humid conditions, botrytis causes a gray, powdery mold to form on flowers. It's a disease that is easily dispersed, so when disposing of affected flowers, they need to be handled delicately, to avoid spreading spores. Treatment with benomyl sprays should be an effective control.

Wilt diseases

There are several wilt diseases, all of which mainly affect perpetual-flowering carnations grown in greenhouses. They are invariably fatal, but most new cultivars have been bred for their high resistance to these and other diseases. Growing plants in pots or "Grobags" resting on straw to prevent contact with any surrounding soil is an effective way of preventing the incidence of wilt diseases.

Bacterial wilt causes plants to wilt suddenly, with the stem brownish and slimy.

Fusarium wilt is a fungal disease. It causes the plant to become stunted and discolored, though the stems do not become slimy.

Verticillium wilt (*Phialophora cinerescens*) is a fungal disease causing leaves to turn straw-colored and side shoots to twist. Broken stems show brown discoloration.

When any wilt disease appears, it is important to act fast to prevent its spread. Affected plants must be removed from the greenhouse and burned as quickly as possible. Surrounding soil needs to be sterilized or discarded, as do any pots in which infected plants are found.

Stem rot

Also called root rot, and difficult to identify, this disease causes stem decay just below the soil surface. The plant suddenly wilts and dies. Avoid infested soil and destroy affected plants. Root rot can be controlled with drenches of benomyl, but it is rarely a problem provided drainage is good and planting is not too deep.

Carnation viruses

Carnation plants frequently carry viral diseases, although many cultivars may show no symptoms. Where leaves are severely mottled or streaked, the plants should be destroyed. Eradicating aphids, which spread viruses, is the best method of control.

Disorders
Calyx splitting

This disorder occurs when the flower is so buxom that as it opens it pushes beyond the natural containment of the calyx. Extreme fluctuations in temperature or overwatering of a dry plant may cause it to happen. It is of concern primarily for commercial growers of perpetual carnations, as it spoils their market value, and for amateurs who plan to exhibit their plants, as blooms with a split calyx are disqualified. The well-known old garden pink 'Mrs. Sinkins' regularly splits her calyxes.

Curly tip

Another disorder of perpetual carnations, this very noticeable problem may appear in midwinter. It causes the growing tips of foliage to curl and distort, but with increasing light and warmth, the condition disappears.

Pinks are easy-care, healthy plants that produce self-seeding colonies where the conditions are right.

CHAPTER 11

Hybridizing

by Dr. Keith Hammett

Breeding new cultivars

The most important feature of any breeding program is a well-defined goal. Indeed, without a goal, any hybridizing or seed saving is no more than a "look-see."

Breeding objectives vary widely. Amateur carnation and pink enthusiasts often seek show-winning qualities or novelty, while commercial breeders serving the cut-flower industry are much more interested in a consistently high yield and disease resistance. However, all conventional breeding programs consist of similar stages:

1. Defining your goal
2. Selecting parent plants
3. How the plants breed
4. Cross-pollination
5. Producing seed
6. Sowing seed and cultivating plants
7. Selecting promising plants
8. Testing and retesting
9. Naming successful plants
10. Sale and distribution
11. Special aims

1. Defining your goal

Generally, people graduate to hybridizing after gaining experience as a gardener and/or exhibitor. This is an important time when growers build up a good knowledge of which cultivars are available and their relative strengths and weaknesses. A keen grower will notice, for example, that many of the laced pinks that have the most distinct markings and win prizes at shows are often the hardest to propagate

A distinctive color scheme.

and die easily if grown in the garden. For this reason, he or she decides that the goal will be to produce a well-laced pink with white ground color that is able to win prizes at shows, but which will also be a good garden plant. Even when not in flower, the plant needs to be attractive and disease free.

2. Selecting parent plants

It is important to take time to select parents; in the long run this will minimize wasted time later in the process. For our laced pink, select those cultivars with the best lacing to act as one parent, and for the second parent look for other plants that may be less well marked or not laced at all, but which have good plant and propagation attributes. In other words, seek plants that have stood the test of time. There is a tendency for people to get caught up in the excitement associated with the latest introductions and to use these in their breeding before the newcomers have had a chance to prove themselves.

Look outside your immediate area or country. Plants closer to your goal may already exist. There is no point in reinventing the wheel. Keep an open mind; sometimes, outstanding plants can be raised from commercially available seed. You might find a good parent that has the added advantage of widening your gene pool. This is sometimes referred to as "bringing in new blood."

Yes, all of this will take time. Breeders do need to think in decades. It will be necessary to make some exploratory crosses. A plant can be a good parent because it produces seed easily or because it produces a high level of worthwhile offspring. One is very lucky to identify plants that do both. Do not jump to conclusions too soon regarding the ability of a plant to produce good progeny. Sometimes, a plant may produce a high level of good offspring in combination with one partner and nothing of value in another combination.

Because dianthus and carnations have a long and mixed parentage, a breeder will tell you they are best thought of as "mongrel swarms." By this they mean that if you cross a perpetual carnation with a perpetual carnation, you are most likely to produce plants which broadly resemble perpetual carnations, but within any population or family resulting from a single cross you will find a wide diversity of characteristics and combinations. With pinks you are likely to encounter an even greater diversity.

Often basic genetics are taught in terms of Mendel's initial experiments, first carried out in the mid-19th century. As these involved green peas and were later expanded by work on sweet peas, they can be very confusing if used to try to explain to a layperson what is happening with a plant like dianthus. Unlike varieties of peas, which can be encouraged to breed true from seed, dianthus are most commonly propagated vegetatively from cuttings, or if sold as seed, the seedlings vary widely within broad parameters.

When breeding dianthus, parents are chosen, crosses made, seed produced and populations or families raised from which individual plants are selected. These selected individual plants are then propagated vegetatively. Such plants, after further trialing and propagation, may be given a name and disseminated. For a pink like 'Far Cry' (syn 'Baby Blanket'), many hundreds of thousands of plants were produced, all of which were essentially the same as the plant first selected.

The important thing for a new breeder to remember is that some traits appear to be controlled by a single gene, while other traits are controlled by a number of genes (polygenes) that work together. Characteristics like simple flower color, such as red or white, appear to be controlled by single genes, while characteristics like flower size or stem length are more likely to be controlled by polygenes.

Even for the simple, single-gene traits, the expression of that trait depends on whether the gene is inherited from both or only one parent. Some characteristics dominate others. If red flowers are fully dominant over white, only red flowers will be expressed in the offspring (F1 generation) when a white-flowered plant is crossed with a red. However, if a number of the red offspring are crossed together (sibcrossed), we might expect at least a few white flowers in the next generation (F2).

Because of these complexities, it is difficult to make accurate predictions. Plant and animal breeding is at least as much art as science. Remember that

Opposite: 'Front Cover', a new border × perennial carnation bred by Keith Hammett and still under trial.

many generations of gardeners and farmers, working long before scientists attempted to explain the processes, produced the cultivated plants that we have now. For these reasons it is essential that breeders work systematically and keep very good records. If they make sure that they only name and distribute plants that are an *improvement* on cultivars already existing, they will make progress.

Pollen on the anthers is bright when fresh and can be white (above) or blue/gray (below).

3. How the plants breed

Some plants have evolved so that they cannot fertilize themselves, such as dahlias, while others like sweet peas have evolved to ensure that they normally only pollinate themselves. Dianthus have the ability to both self- and cross-pollinate. This makes life easier, as it offers a range of breeding strategies.

It is important when starting to hybridize any plant to first gain an understanding of its breeding mechanisms. Dianthus flowers consist of both **male and female parts**. Wild dianthus normally have single flowers with five petals. The male parts are the **anthers,** which produce pollen. These mature first and pollen is shed well before the female parts are mature. This means that a flower is unlikely to pollinate itself, but it is possible to self-pollinate by using flowers at different stages of development on the same plant.

The female part is the **stigma**, which usually consists of two goat-like horns covered in hairs when mature. These grow progressively until they become curled and, unlike many flowers where the receptive area is limited, pollination can take place over much of their surface. They are receptive from the time well-developed hairs can be seen on their surface and they start to curve significantly.

4. Cross-pollination

Pollination is simple. Take an anther that has recently split and is covered in fresh pollen and dab this over a selected, receptive stigma. Pollen varies in color from white to almost blue and is bright when fresh, becoming dull as it ages. Use the freshest pollen possible. It can be easily seen after it has been put on the stigma.

There is little fear of self-pollination from the same flowers, so there is no need to remove the anthers from a flower chosen to be a mother or seed producer. As well, unless there is a lot of insect activity (which might lead to unwanted cross-pollination), there is probably no need to cover blooms. If you have limited facilities and want to make

1. Mature anthers coated in pollen are visible surrounding the still short, straight stigma which is not yet mature.

2. On this flower the curled stigma shows it has reached maturity.

3. Fresh pollen is applied to the receptive mature stigmas.

4. The flower collapses 24 hours after pollination while the unpollinated flowers of the same age remain fresh.

absolutely sure that there are no unknown fathers contributing to your seedling population, cover the bloom before and after pollination with a bag, made preferably from nylon or a similar synthetic material. It is important to have air movement to minimize fungal attack. Do not use plastic bags which "sweat."

In dianthus the flower collapses within 24 hours of pollination, so it is easy to know if fertilization has been successful. It is for this reason that keen exhibitors remove the developing stigmas from

5. Well-developed seed pod.

Breeding parents in the quest for a garden-worthy yellow dianthus: *Dianthus knappii* is the small yellow bloom, 'Far North' the large, white one. The offspring, or F1 hybrid, is large and cream-colored.

their prize blooms to stop any stray pollination and disaster.

With double flowers, many of the extra petals have been formed from anthers and you can observe petals that have parts of anthers attached. It is often very difficult to find pollen in the exceedingly double flowers, and it is one of life's ironies that the most desirable plants are frequently reluctant parents.

The number of seeds formed in a seed pod varies with the cultivar. In some, very few are formed, while in others a hundred or more may be obtained. Often this depends on growing conditions and reflects the number of successful fertilizations. If a lot of ovules have been fertilized, the pod will develop as a distinct, elongated cylinder to accommodate the developing seed.

5. Producing seed

Once fertilization has been successful, the breeder changes from being a flower grower to a fruit grower. A few days after the flower has collapsed, the faded petals should be removed to avoid infection by fungi, and if a bag has been used, this should not be replaced.

A week or so later, it is wise to remove the calyx surrounding the developing pod, also for reasons of hygiene, and it is a good idea to apply a fungicide. Depending on the conditions, pods usually reach maturity about a month after pollination. When they start to change from green to straw-colored, remove them from the plant, put them in a paper bag and place the bag in a warm, dry place like a sunny windowsill.

When the pods are dry, open them at the top and shake out the seeds. It is a good idea to split them open and pick out any remaining seeds with tweezers. Seeds are usually nearly black in color, but can also fade to nearly white. They are flat and flake-like and can be sown immediately or stored.

Store seeds in cool, dark conditions. It is possible to successfully store seeds for many years by placing them in envelopes inside sealed food-storage containers in a deep freeze operating at -2°F (-18°C).

6. Sowing seed and cultivating plants

Professional breeders have a different viewpoint than the home gardener who likely expects every plant raised to contribute positively to the garden display. Each cross between two specific parents produces a family of offspring or a population from which the breeder hopes to identify individual plants that fulfil his or her goal, or at least are a step closer to that goal than their parents.

Seed-raising is easy, as was discussed in Chapter 9 on propagation (see page 69). Plants are best cultivated in an area like a vegetable garden and arranged in rows. Think of it as a workshop, rather than a display area. However good your selection of parents, every population will have a proportion of plants that are worse than their parents. You can only expect a few which will be superior. Many novice breeders have a tendency to think that all their babies are winners. Learn to be objective and ask yourself "if another breeder had produced this plant, would I be prepared to spend good money to buy it?"

7. Selecting promising plants

Even the most double parents (those plants that have complex flowers with several overlapping layers of petals) produce a proportion of single flowered offspring (that is, plants that have only one layer of petals, which do not overlap). For carnations, these are known traditionally as "jacks" and can be removed as soon as they flower. In fact, they can be recognized before they open, as they have long, thin buds. Equally, a proportion will be "splitters" or "bursters"—flowers with too many petals and a split calyx. These have very rounded or nearly spherical buds and should also be discarded. The quicker you get rid of the trash, the easier it is to see what remains of value.

It is a good idea to have plants of the parent types growing near the seedling beds to act as reference plants. It is impossible to make objective comparisons from memory.

With experience you will learn which individuals in a population have potential. Mark these with a tall, clearly visible cane and when you have decided which warrant further testing, give the

plant a code to identify them. Remember, though, that at this stage all you are saying is that "these plants warrant further testing."

8. Testing and retesting

Further testing is important before names are applied and plants disseminated. Don't rush to "leave your thumbprint on history" and name a plant too soon. Many plants are introduced each year, never to be heard of again.

Take cuttings of selected, coded plants and keep records regarding how well they propagate. At least ten plants of each selection is recommended so that the selection may be tested in a number of different positions in the garden and perhaps in containers as well.

Many pinks form neat, mounded plants when young, only to open out or go bald in the center as they get older. Several seasons of testing are essential to assess performance of traits like these. Similarly, a young seedling may produce good quality flowers in its first season, never to be matched subsequently, while others settle down and improve with age.

As with all things, balance is required. All cultivars have a finite useful life, so it is important not to vacillate too long before making a decision regarding naming and release. A good rule of thumb is that "if a breeder is not sure whether a plant is worth naming, it is not!"

As for a variety's longevity, remember that most plants bearing long-established names are almost all impostors of much more recent origin.

9. Naming successful plants

The naming of cultivated plants is covered by the *International Code of Nomenclature for Cultivated Plants*. The most recent edition was published in 1995. The code contains guidelines to be followed when applying a name. The International Registration Authority for Dianthus is the Royal Horticultural Society in the U.K. It is a good idea to apply for registration of your proposed name before you start using it. As there are many thousands of names already registered, it can sometimes be difficult to find one that has not already been used, which explains why some amateur breeders often use prefix names to identify their creations (e.g., 'Oakwood Ann Colville', 'Oakwood Clara Boole').

10. Sale and distribution

In today's market-led world, image and packaging rule. The days of specialist nurseries devoted to a single genus are almost gone. This can make it difficult for an essentially amateur breeder to market his or her creations.

Occasionally, an amateur's product will have commercial potential, and there are an increasing numbers of people who act as agents. Few nurseries worldwide invest in specific breeding programs, so there are always people on the lookout to see what they might pick up. Agents can be very helpful here, especially where it is deemed appropriate to protect the product with Plant Patents, Plant Variety Rights or Plant Breeders' Rights, depending upon the country.

The enthusiast cum breeder will most likely need to accept more modest distribution of his or her creations. This is often accomplished by propagating a limited number of plants and advertising directly in specialist publications or gardening magazines and on the Internet. If your aim is to share your plants, make a contribution to the fabric of recreational horticulture and perhaps cover some of your costs, this can work well.

11. Special aims

It is relatively easy to simply stir the existing gene pool and to refine existing forms. This is important and valuable in itself because, as mentioned, individual cultivars have a finite life. In periods when many people are interested in breeding, a genus improves; in periods of neglect, forms are lost and the plant pool degenerates.

The production of new forms and the re-creation of forms that previously existed are much more difficult. An example of a type now lost to cultivation is the bizarre carnation, where two or more colors were flaked onto a white ground. It is tantalizing to browse through some of the books published early in the 19th century and realize just what has been lost.

Few flowers have a full spectrum of color pigments—*Dianthus* lacks yellow. While the carnation has yellow varieties, pinks do not, despite attempts over a very long time to achieve this. The only easily accessible *Dianthus* species with yellow pigmentation is *D. knappii*. There are some rare African species with yellow flowers, but these are very different from other dianthus and they have proven difficult to establish in cultivation.

Dianthus knappii was at one time thought to be the source of yellow carnations, a view strengthened by this species having 30 chromosomes, like the carnation. However, pigment analysis quickly established that the yellow color in *D. knappii* is attributable to flavonoid pigments, while carnations are yellow because of chalcone. Chalcone is a chemical, which by the action of a series of enzymes as the flowers develop changes progressively to the red and blue anthocyanin pigments. These pigments give pinks their pink and mauve shades.

The reason there are yellow carnations is because a mutation has occurred that has turned off the chemical mechanism that changes the yellow chalcone into anthocyanins, and chalcone accumulates in the flowers. Whenever pinks are crossed with yellow carnations the mechanism that changes chalcone to anthocyanin is re-established and the offspring are always pink or mauve.

An alternative approach, attempted many times, has been to cross *Dianthus knappii* with pinks. It has been possible to produce cream-colored pinks, but *D. knappii* has a very poor plant habit, which its offspring inherit. As pinks have 90 chromosomes, any attempt to backcross onto pinks with good habit

'Cloud Nine', a popular Hammett hybrid.

quickly loses the yellow coloring. Equally, back-crossing onto *D. knappii* to intensify the yellow pigmentation only makes the plant habit worse.

A similar situation exists with regard to border carnations. Some colors and color combinations are unique to this flower. Attempts to introduce similar coloring into pinks with good habit and repeat-flowering attributes have so far failed, again because in pink/carnation crosses there are three times as many pink chromosomes as there are carnation chromosomes and these swamp the carnation genome. In addition, some of the most spectacular colorings found in border carnations are recessive characteristics, which makes their expression even more difficult.

An understanding of some basic scientific information like this can help a breeder know when he or she is on a wrong course while sometimes it can reveal how to overcome the problem.

APPENDIX

Sources of Plants

The importation of live plants and plant materials across borders requires special arrangements, which will be detailed in suppliers' catalogs.

American regulations vary according to the country of origin and type of plant. Every order requires a phytosanitary certificate and may require a CITES (Convention on International Trade in Endangered Species of Wild Fauna and Flora) certificate. For more information contact:
USDA-APHIS-PPQ
Permit Unit
4700 River Road, Unit 136
Riverdale, Maryland 20727-1236
Tel: (301) 734-8645
Fax: (301) 734-5786
Website: www.aphis.udsda.gov

Canadians importing plant material must pay a fee and complete an "application for permit to import."
Contact:
Plant Health and Production Division
Canadian Food Inspection Agency
2nd Floor West, Permit Office
59 Camelot Drive
Nepean, Ontario K1A 0Y9
Tel: (613) 225-2342
Fax: (613) 228-6605
Website: www.cfia-agr.ca

Aimers
81 Temperance Street
Aurora, Ontario L4G 2R1
Tel: (905) 841-6226
Fax: (905) 727-7333
Seeds for English strains of carnations and pinks. Ships to the U.S.

Bluestone Perennials
7211 Middle Ridge Road
Madison, Ohio 44057
Toll-free Tel: 1-800-852-5243
Fax: (440) 428-7198
E-mail: bluestone@bluestoneperennials.com
Website: www.bluestoneperennials.com
Good selection of Allwood-type pinks, Cheddars, maiden pinks. Does not ship to Canada.

Canyon Creek Nursery
3527 Dry Creek Road
Oroville, California 95965
Tel: (530) 533-2166
Website: www.canyoncreeknursery.com
Good selection of heirloom pinks. Does not ship to Canada.

Corn Hill Nursery
2700 Route 890
Corn Hill, New Brunswick E4Z 1M2
Tel: (506) 756-3635
Fax: (506) 756-1087
Website: www.cornhillnursery.com
Good selection. Does not ship perennials to the U.S.

Flower Scent Gardens
14820 Moine Road
Doylestown, Ohio 44230-9744
Tel: (330) 658-5946
Website: www.flowerscentgardens.com
Good selection of antique pinks and scented carnations. Does not ship to Canada.

Goodwin Creek Gardens
P.O. Box 83
Williams, Oregon 97544-0083
Tel: (541) 846-7357
Toll-free Tel: 1-800-846-7359
Website: www.goodwincreekgardens.com
Excellent selection of heirloom pinks, including the rare double 'Bridal Veil'.

Jackson and Perkins
P.O. Box 1028
Medford, Oregon 97501
Tel: (877) 456-8800
Toll-free Fax: 1-800-242-0329
E-mail: mcady@bco.com
Website: www.jacksonandperkins.com
Pinks and border carnations.

JDS Gardens
R. R. #4
2277 County Road 20
Harrow, Ontario N0R 1G0
Tel: (519) 738-9513
Fax: (519) 738-3539
E-mail: info@jdsgardens.com
Website: www.jdsgardens.com
Selection of dianthus cultivars.

Nora's Nursery
5761 Cape George Road
Port Townsend, WA 98368
Tel/Fax: (360) 379-3920
Website: www.norasnursery.com
Excellent selection of antique pinks.

The Perennial Gardens
13139 224th Street
Maple Ridge, British Columbia V4R 2P6
Tel: (604) 467-4218
Fax: (604) 467-3181
Website: www.perennialgardener.com
Wide selection of carnations and pinks. Does not ship to U.S.

Plant Delights Nursery
9241 Sauls Road
Raleigh, North Carolina 27603
Tel: (919) 772-4794
Website: www.plantdelights.com
Excellent catalog available for 10 34-cent stamps or a box of chocolates.

Specialty Perennials
481 Reflection Road
Apple Valley, Minnesota 55124
Tel: (612) 432-8673
Fax: (612) 342-8673
E-mail: meum71@aol.com
Website: www.hardyplants.com
Wide selection of dianthus seed.

Stokes Seeds Inc.
Box 548
Buffalo, New York 14220-0548
Toll-free Tel: (800) 396-9238
Website: www.stokeseeds.com
Excellent selection of modern pinks, carnations and sweet Williams.

Sunny Border Nurseries, Inc.
1709 Kensington Road
P.O. Box 483
Kensington, Connecticut 06037
Tel: (860) 828-0321
Fax: (860) 828-9318
Website: www.sunnyborder.com
Wide selection of dianthus cultivars.

Sunnyslope Gardens
8638 Huntington Drive
San Gabriel, California 91775
Tel: (626) 287-4071]
Website: www.sunnyslopegardens.com
Good mail-order source for perpetual-flowering carnations.

White Flower Farm
Route 63
Litchfield, Connecticut 06759-0050
Toll-free Tel: 1-800-503-9624
Fax: (860) 482-0532
Website: www.whiteflowerfarm.com
Wide selection of perennials, including dianthus.

Wrightman Alpines
Route 3, 1503 Napperton Drive
Naperton, Ontario N0M 2B0
Tel/Fax: (519) 247-3751
Website: www.golden.net/~wrightman
Good selection of dianthus. Ships to the U.S.

Societies

North American Cottage Garden Society/
North American Dianthus Society
c/o Ms. Denis Garrett
Membership Secretary
NACGS/NADS
P.O. Box 188
Peagram, Tennessee 37143-0188
E-mail: randbear@nets.com
Publishes quarterly magazine, Small Honesties, *and organizes seed exchanges.*

Bibliography

Allwood, Montagu C. *Carnations and All Dianthus.* London: Allwood Bros. Ltd, 1926.

Cobbett, William. *The English Gardener.* London: Bloomsbury, 1996. (First published 1829.)

Dick, J. Harrison (ed.). *Commercial Carnation Culture.* London: A.T. De la Mare Printing and Publishing Co. Ltd., 1915.

Galbally, John with Eileen Galbally. *Carnations and Pinks for Garden and Greenhouse.* Portland: Timber Press, 1997.

Gatt, Melanie Kaye, "Cytogenetics and Hybridisation in the Genus *Dianthus L.*" Unpublished M.Sc. thesis, University of Auckland, New Zealand, 1995.

Gould, Jim. "Laced Pinks." London: *Hortus* 1992 6:2, pp. 38–41.

Hakansson, Lennard. *The Carnation Propagators' Association History, 1962–1987.* Unpublished. Denmark, 1987.

Harvey, John H. "Gilliflowers and Carnations." London: *Garden History Society Publication,* 1993.

Jarratt, Joy. *Growing Carnations* (2nd ed.). Kenthurst, NSW: Kangaroo Press, 1996.

Lloyd, Christopher. *The Well-Tempered Garden.* London: Viking, 1985.

New Zealand Gardener. Various articles. May, 1997; September 1997.

Phillips, Roger and Rix, Martyn. *Perennials.* Vol 2. London: Macmillan, 1991.

Robinson, William. *The English Flower Garden.* London: Bloomsbury, 1996. (First published 1883.)

Smith, Fred C. A *Plantsman's Guide to Carnations and Pinks.* London Ward Lock Ltd., 1990.

Whiten, Faith and Geoff. *Making a Cottage Garden.* London: Harper Collins, 1993.

Index